This wise, pithy and godly advice, given with grace and humility by pastors' wives for other pastors' wives, is also applicable to all married Christian women, both young and older.
Faith Cook, author and speaker

What an honest, stimulating, life-affirming book! The writers have chalked up several hundred years of experience and practical wisdom between them. When they speak about living by grace as ministers' wives, they really know what they are talking about. This should be mandatory reading for all ministers' wives and everyone who wants to know how to encourage them.
Marcus Honeysett, Director of Living Leadership

Packed with wisdom, this book will bring refreshed vision and encouragement to many clergy wives. I found the teaching on juggling children and ministry, handling criticism and finding a healthy sense of 'self' as a minister's wife particularly helpful. If only this book had been available when at the age of twenty-one I married a trainee vicar, many of my questions would have been answered.
Lucinda van der Hart, co-author of The Pregnancy Book *and* Soul Food for Mums

The Minister's Wife

The Minister's Wife

Privileges, Pressures & Pitfalls

Ann Benton and friends

ivp

INTER-VARSITY PRESS
Norton Street, Nottingham NG7 3HR, England
Email: ivp@ivpbooks.com
Website: www.ivpbooks.com

First published 2011

British Library Cataloguing in Publication Data
A catalogue record for this book is available from the British Library.

ISBN: 978–1–84474–556–2

Set in Dante 12/15pt
Typeset in Great Britain by CRB Associates, Potterhanworth, Lincolnshire
Printed and bound in Great Britain by Ashford Colour Press Ltd, Gosport,
Hampshire

Inter-Varsity Press publishes Christian books that are true to the Bible and that
communicate the gospel, develop discipleship and strengthen the church for its
mission in the world.

Inter-Varsity Press is closely linked with the Universities and Colleges Christian
Fellowship, a student movement connecting Christian Unions in universities and
colleges throughout Great Britain, and a member movement of the International
Fellowship of Evangelical Students. Website: www.uccf.org.uk

From the Platform

I have the suit, the smile, and there I stand;
I modulate my voice, use pace and pause,
Speak from the notes clutched in my trembling hand
And crave the approbation and applause.

But afterwards I cringe with guilty shame –
'If they could all my faults and failures see . . . '
I know that one can have too good a name,
And fear that they should think too well of me.

By rights one day someone will find me out
And heap upon my head some wretched curse.
Denial? Revenge? 'No, no,' I ought to shout –
'If you knew all – I really am much worse.'

Then I recall there was a time, a place
When He became a curse, and I found grace.

© Ann Benton

Contents

Introduction

'I could write a book . . . '

How many times in thirty years have I muttered those words to myself?

Ministers' wives appear in fiction. Anthony Trollope painted some famously unflattering portraits in his *Chronicles of Barsetshire*. He found the juxtaposition between preaching the kingdom of heaven and handling life on earth a rich vein for comedy, as others have done since. There are incongruities about life in the manse or the vicarage. The minster is sometimes regarded as a separate category of human being, and so too is his wife.

The stereotypes remain, and probably strike fear into any twenty-first-century woman about to embark on ministry life. Barbara Pym in her 1953 novel *Jane and Prudence* describes a woman not at all comfortable with what she sees as the expectations of her role: ' . . . clergy wives have to be very careful, you know. They have to be sitting there in their dowdy old clothes in a pew rather too near the front – it's a kind of duty.'

That sentiment, if taken seriously, certainly needs challenging. But it also raises a reasonable question. What, if any, *are* the duties of clergy wives? You could fill several shelves with books about being a minister – no shortage of advice and inspiration there – but a minister's wife? She must largely find her own way through the rotas and the teapots.

So when I was contacted by the Women's Ministry Team of the FIEC (The Fellowship of Independent Evangelical Churches) and asked to submit a chapter towards a book by and for ministers' wives, I was only too happy to oblige. Later I contributed a second chapter, and finally somehow the whole project landed in my lap.

So this is a book about life as a ministry wife. It aims to inform, prepare and inspire those who are, or who might become, fellow members of that peculiar group of women whom my husband calls 'heroines'.

The original concept was that chapters would be solicited from a range of ministers' wives. Contrary to popular misconception, we are not all the same, and our various experiences and backgrounds colour our take on the role. So there are many voices in this book. Some are women who see themselves as front-line, full-time co-workers with their husbands; others would look on themselves more as backroom support. Some knew from the outset of their marriage that this would be their path and fully embraced it; some expected one kind of life and found themselves in another. Some have substantial employment outside the church and home; others do not. All have known pain, misunderstanding and struggle, as well as pleasure, purpose and fulfilment.

Apart from all being married to men who serve full-time in preaching/pastoral ministry, the writers have two things in common. First, we are all evangelical Christians. That is to say, we believe in the Bible as the inerrant Word of God; we believe that Jesus died on the cross to make complete atonement for our sins; we believe that we are saved by faith alone in Christ alone. Secondly, we are all complementarian on the question of gender. That is to say, we believe that God made male and female equal but different. In family life and in the church, God intends male headship, after the pattern of Christ who loved the church and gave himself for her. A wife is to be her husband's helper and to submit to his loving and sacrificial leadership. However, readers who take issue with the evangelical, complementarian standpoint may still value the insights in this book while disagreeing with some of its explanations and applications.

In most cases the various writers were assigned their subject. They wrote their chapters without seeing what the other women had written. What was interesting to me as the editor was that, despite our differences, there was a very large area of agreement on, for example, the kind of sins that stalk the manse. This called for some ruthless editorial lopping, in the interest of avoiding tedious repetition. Nonetheless there will still be some central themes which emerge several times but need to be restated in the respective contexts, precisely because they are so dominant. Let the reader understand and forgive. Most already in ministry will do so.

My heartfelt thanks go to all the contributors for their patience and humility as the scripts went back and forth in cyberspace. The writers are all women whose hearts beat with a passion for God's kingdom. They are grateful to IVP for the opportunity to disseminate this collection. One of the reasons why I and others were so keen to see this kind of resource in print is a kingdom reason. There is a tragic loss to the churches year on year of many gifted men who embark on ministerial life and give up. Of course, there is a wide range of circumstances behind the statistics. But one common reason why a man steps down from leadership in the church is that his job was making his wife deeply unhappy. She had no idea it would be like that. Or she cannot handle the unwritten expectations of a church. Or, or, or . . . No godly man wants to see his wife spiral into resentment or resigned misery because of his chosen path in life. The writers humbly hope that, by their combined offering of the wisdom of Scripture and experience, this book will serve to keep men in gospel ministry.

My husband often reflects on the comments of Stephen Ambrose, an eminent American World War 2 historian. Ambrose records that Hitler's army had much better military equipment than the Allies had. Technologically it was state of the art. But when the German tanks got damaged, they were just left to rust. The Allies on the other hand had a team of mechanics ready to rescue and repair their damaged tanks and turn them round to be back on the battlefield in a very short time. This, alleges Ambrose, was one of the secrets of the Allies' ultimate success in Europe after the D-day landings.

Gospel ministry is a war, and men get wounded. A man can sometimes return to his manse or vicarage on a Sunday night or after a church meeting completely shot up. The mainten-ance and repair supplied by a minister's wife is essential to his return to the front line. That is the kingdom importance of the minister's wife.

Ann Benton, February 2011

1. Her responsibility to God: 'Daughter, do you love me?'

by Val Archer

Val had godly parents who taught and modelled the gospel to her from her earliest years. Today she is married to Trevor, and they have four children, now grown up, and a beloved grandson.

For over forty years, Trevor and Val worked for Chessington Evangelical Church, and for twenty-five of those years Trevor was the pastor. Val looks back on that time as an immensely happy one and, despite the normal quota of struggles and difficulties, considers it a huge privilege to have served there. Having both been in the church since childhood, it was with quite sad hearts that she and Trevor left the leadership team in January 2011 for Trevor to take up the post of Training Director with FIEC. However, in this new venture Val greatly looks forward to meeting up with and encouraging many ministry wives and students throughout the country. Happily, she and Trevor are able to remain in Chessington,

> where Val will continue her 'friendship ministry', mainly
> in the coffee shops of local garden centres. Her delights
> are looking after grandson Oliver, playing the piano and
> gardening, when she is not working as a medical secretary
> in a busy local hospital.

When asked what one piece of advice she would give Christian
women today, Helen Roseveare, one of the great missionaries
of the twentieth century, had no hesitation in responding:
'Do you love Jesus?' Her reply echoed Jesus' challenge to Peter
in John 21 after the resurrection. Before Jesus could talk to
Peter about his future ministry, he needed to ask Peter whether
or not he loved him. Love for Jesus takes us to the very heart
of Christian discipleship.

We need to understand at the outset of this book that the
relationship of a minister's wife to Jesus Christ is *the* pivotal
thing which will impact on every other area of her life and
ministry.

When the Saviour set his heart upon us before the foundation of the world, it was so that we might be in a precious
relationship with him, a relationship of love and devotion. It
was so that we might be regularly refreshed in him. And all
that we are flows from this intimate bond.

Knowing about Christ alone will not do. Working for him
will not do. A minister's wife is called into a personal, living,
ongoing fellowship with him, not because her husband has
prominence in the church, but because of who she is in Christ
and all he calls her to. Busyness is no substitute for refreshment in Christ, zeal no substitute for love for Christ, personal
commitment no substitute for contentment with Christ.

How easy it is to allow our activity *for* the Saviour to take
the place of our devotion *to* him. It is far easier to be dashing

around, crossing things off our action lists, than spending time with him and turning our thoughts to him throughout the day.

Unwittingly, a minister's wife can find herself modelling a grotesque distortion of discipleship in which busyness is equated with godliness, duty supplanting devotion. I know; I've been there. For years I gave completely the wrong message to the women in our church family, frantically trying to be involved with every person and every activity, to the neglect of my own walk with the Lord. I thank God that he has given me the opportunity publicly to apologize for that appalling imbalance and time to redress it in recent years.

Martyn Lloyd-Jones wrote:

> The man [or woman] who knows the love of Christ in his heart can do more in one hour than the busy type of man can do in a century. God forbid that we should ever make activity an end in itself. Let us realise that the motive must come first and that the motive must ever be the love of Christ.[1]

We are reminded every time we come to the Lord's Table or communion that our Lord asks us to 'take' from him before we engage in service for him. 'Take, eat.' He doesn't ask us to 'do' before we have 'taken'. Whose we are is infinitely more important than what we do.

Church history contains countless stories of men and women who gave sacrificially of themselves, in many cases to the extent of premature death, for the sake of the gospel. But what marked them out was their motivation and their resources. They were motivated by love of their Lord and they drew from the deep well of God's Word and his strength, and it is their example we should follow today. Think of Ann Hasseltine who, in October 1810 as a twenty-year-old living in New England, was considering the proposal of marriage from Adoniram Judson, a man whose heart was set on foreign mission. She writes in her journal:

> If nothing in providence appears to prevent, I must spend my days in a heathen land. I am a creature of God, and he has an undoubted right to do with me, as seems good in his sight . . . He has my heart in his hands, and when I am called to face danger, to pass through scenes of terror and distress, he can inspire me with fortitude, and enable me to trust in him. Jesus is faithful; his promises are precious.[2]

Throughout the remainder of her life, serving the Lord alongside her husband in Burma, Ann proved God's faithfulness and his precious promises. At the age of thirty-seven she passed into the presence of her Lord, having never recovered from a fever that would leave little daughter Marie motherless and husband Adoniram a widower.

You will soon realize that there are very few specific references to ministers' wives in this chapter. That is intentional. It is who we are in Christ, not what we do for him, that matters most. It's all about our *relationship*, not our *role*, and that means that the issues we consider in this chapter apply to every Christian woman who aspires to be godly, regardless of what she does in the church.

You will only be able to fulfil the responsibilities of a minister's wife, or indeed of any God-given assignment, if your personal walk with the Lord is the thing that is sustaining you. You will soon realize that you will only be able to deal with criticism, handle pressures or recognize the privileges that are yours as a minister's wife, if you constantly apply the gospel of grace to your life.

We're going to look at eight reasons why our relationship with God is so vital.

Our relationship with the Lord is *the* most important thing in our lives because . . .

a. It is our calling to be holy

In the great sweep of the eternal plan recorded in Ephesians 1, Paul reminds us that God has blessed us with every spiritual blessing in Christ: he set his heart upon us before the foundation of the world; he welcomed us into his family as his adopted children; he poured his love and grace and mercy on us. But when he did these things, he did not call us primarily to a life of service; rather to a life of relationship with him, so that we might 'know him better' (verse 17).

We need that same gospel to speak into our lives every day, because every day we face the temptation to move away from the cross and leave the God who first called us.

God's desire for us is that we should be holy in character, just as he is holy in character, so that all the Christlike characteristics we see in him will be formed in us. 1 Peter 1:15–16 reminds us: 'Just as he who called you is holy, so be holy in all you do; for it is written: "Be holy, because I am holy."' We have been called to a life of holiness. As daughters of the King, we are to be those women, whose 'delight is in the law of the LORD . . . like a tree planted by streams of water' (Psalm 1:2–3). This is the calling of every Christian, whether man or woman.

Our relationship with the Lord is *the* most important thing in our lives because . . .

b. It is to be our greatest joy

In his book *Finding Joy*, Marcus Honeysett writes, 'Grace is so wonderful, that receiving it leads to joy as night follows day. It is impossible to taste something so delightful and not enjoy it and be stirred up to worship God.'[3] So many of us 'know' the truth of the good news of grace, but fail to reckon on it in our lives and own it for ourselves.

Marcus continues, 'Let's preach it to our hearts that we stand in the truth of God's grace. Let's consider it to be true about ourselves and be glad. This is who we are: grace people! It is our identity in Christ.'[4]

George Müller is famous for having established orphanages in Bristol, while joyfully depending on God for all his needs. In 1841 he made a life-changing discovery:

> I saw more clearly than ever that the first, great and primary business to which I ought to attend every day was, to have my soul happy in the Lord. The first thing to be concerned about was not, how much I might serve the Lord, how I might glorify the Lord; but how I might get my soul into a happy state, and how my inner man might be nourished . . . Now I saw that the most important thing I had to do was to give myself to the reading of the Word of God and to meditation on it, that thus my heart might be comforted, encouraged, warned, reproved, instructed; and that thus, whilst meditating, my heart might be brought into communion with the Lord.[5]

Like George Müller, we are to be those who, while delighting ourselves in the Lord and his Word, acknowledge our utter dependence on our Saviour. In 2 Peter 3:18 the apostle exhorts us to 'grow in the grace and knowledge of our Lord and Saviour Jesus Christ'. We cannot grow our heart's affection for the Lord without growing our delight in his Word. His Word is the means by which he has chosen to make himself known to us. Like the two disciples who met Jesus after his resurrection on the road to Emmaus, we will find that it is his words that cause our hearts to burn within us. His Word shapes our life, makes us wise unto salvation, moulds our thoughts and brings us peace and joy.

Our relationship with the Lord is *the* most important thing in our lives because . . .

c. It is an admission that we need God's help

Moses had been leading the Israelites for over forty years. Just before his death he reminded them to 'take to heart all the words by which I am warning you today . . . For it is no empty word for you, but *your very life*' (Deuteronomy 32:46–47 ESV, italics mine). We need that reminder too. The very Word that quickened our hearts into new birth is the same Word that will give us wisdom and strength for every situation we will face in life and in ministry. It is the Word that gives us hope, makes us wise, gives us assurance and overcomes the evil one. If we sideline our reading and meditating on it through activity and bustle, we do so at our peril.

Reading God's Word leads us naturally to prayer, as our hearts are renewed by the truth and our thoughts once again filled with the things of God. How many times have we just not known *what* or *how* to pray, until we have turned to the Scriptures or to a hymn book and our hearts have been flooded with the truth of the gospel once again? I have always found it most helpful to have copies of a hymn book, *The Book of Common Prayer* and *The Valley of Vision: A Collection of Puritan Prayers and Devotions*[6] close to hand when beginning my time with the Lord. Invariably if I go straight to prayer, the focus is so often on the details of the circumstances surrounding me at that particular time. But reading God's Word, together with these other books, helps centre my thoughts on the far greater plan of God's purposes for the world and those for whom I am praying.

Prayer is not getting God to change his mind to do what we want, but rather aligning our hearts and minds to *his* will. Prayer is the admission that we are desperate for his help and powerless to do anything without him. Prayer is the tangible expression of our need of, and dependence upon, the Lord's help. Conversely, prayerlessness has, at its root, pride. Although we would never verbalize it this way, if we fail to pray, we are actually saying that we can manage quite well without God or his wisdom.

John Piper suggests: 'Prayer is the essential activity of waiting for God – acknowledging our helplessness and his power, calling upon him for help, seeking his counsel . . . Prayer is the antidote for the disease of self-confidence.' He continues, 'God is not looking for people to work for him, so much as he is looking for people who will let him work for them.'[7]

It has been our experience as a couple time after time that, when we have been our most broken, at the end of our own resources and in most desperate need of God's help, that that was precisely when we have known the Lord's blessing and sustenance in an extraordinary way. A number of years ago my personal life was hit by a variety of significant events. Sadness, illness, misunderstanding and perplexing circumstances seemed to crowd in from every side and bring my family humbly to the end of our own resources. While sharing these events openly with the fellowship, many bore testimony to being particularly blessed by Trevor's preaching at that time, and we were able to minister to people at a far deeper level than we had ever known before. Individuals felt that we were able to empathize with them far more because we were sharing similar struggles and difficulties. So, while it was undoubtedly a *hard* time, in God's providence it was a *good* time, which was of great blessing to the fellowship as a whole.

How often sermons prepared and delivered with heavy hearts and tear-stained faces are invariably those that the Lord, in his grace and mercy, uses most powerfully for his glory. We prove yet again that, 'My [God's] grace is sufficient for you, for my power is made perfect in weakness . . . For when I am weak, then I am strong' (2 Corinthians 12:9, 10b).

Our relationship with the Lord is *the* most important thing in our lives because . . .

d. It exposes our sinful hearts

Getting closer to Jesus is not a cosy or comfortable experience, as Peter discovered (John 18). Sooner or later, the Lord will put his finger on those things in our hearts that come before him and actually keep him at a distance. Though we don't realize it, these things are our 'idols', substitutes for God himself.

Idolatry is anything that we believe we need, apart from Jesus, to make us happy or fulfilled. An idol materializes when we desire or pursue something more than we desire Jesus, and when we put our trust in anything other than God. And while we would never admit it, invariably self is at the very centre of our idolatry. Even good things, such as our family, our ministry, our evangelism, our hospitality, our gifts, can become idols when they start to rule our lives.

Particularly common in ministry is the temptation of the three Ps and a C: pride, perfectionism, people-pleasing and comparison. All of these will be unpacked in later chapters of this book. All I will say here from my own experience is that many, many times I have been driven, not by a love of the Lord and his glory or care for his people, but by pride, perfectionism and a desire to please people. I have wanted my reputation and my ministry to be the most successful and acclaimed. Indeed, I have always wanted people to be well disposed towards me. I have compared myself and my situation to others and been full of envy and self-pity.

And it is only as we allow the Holy Spirit's challenging light to expose sinful thought-patterns and attitudes that he will begin the gloriously liberating, if not painful, work of sanctification and transformation. I have found that every day, like the prodigal son, I have needed to 'come to my senses' and return to the Father in repentance and faith. Every day I am like the elder son and need to repent of the self-righteousness and resentment that blind me to the treasure I have always had in my heavenly Father's love and devotion.

Having been a Christian for over half a century, I am so thankful to God for exposing the indwelling sin, deep pride and judgmental spirit in my own heart in a completely new way through two inspiring books, *Gospel Transformation*[8] and *The Enemy Within*.[9] I really cannot commend these publications too highly.

Our relationship with the Lord is *the* most important thing in our lives because . . .

e. It will enable us to be the 'ezer': the strong helper

In God's perfect created order, God made woman to be a 'suitable helper' for her husband. (More on this in chapter two.) Likewise, we are to be our husband's 'ezer', his strong helper, and only a close walking relationship with the Lord will enable us to fulfil that role. There will undoubtedly be times when you are called to be the 'strong helper' for your husband – times that only you know about, of illness, depression, loneliness or unjust criticism. It is at such times that you will need to be the one who ministers to your husband and reminds him of the truths which he has regularly preached to his Christian family.

Over the years, many ministers have testified to the fact that they would have given up during difficult and painful situations in their own lives and churches, had it not been for the spiritual strength and insight of their wives. In each case the wife has indeed been the 'ezer' whose foundation was firmly placed in the Lord. I remember a minister telling of a time when he was in anguish as the church that he had pastored for many years went through a turbulent season, with unrest and discord among some members, and his ministry being undermined by others. After one particularly disagreeable church meeting, his wife determined not to talk about all that had happened, but chose instead to read Psalm 145 to him, reminding him of God's faithfulness and might. He testified to the fact that her strength and godliness at the precise moment of his despair were pivotal in renewing his resolve to trust God afresh and continue ministering to that particular church, where he remains as minister to this day.

It may well be that you will be your husband's 'ezer' simply by keeping family life as calm as possible and making life straightforward for him, so that he can give himself whole-heartedly to the work of ministry. This is an incredibly sacrificial gift which requires godly strength and grace.

During the course of your ministry you will undoubtedly spend hundreds of evenings on your own, have family holidays disrupted, see many arrangements left in tatters, simply because your husband is serving the people God has entrusted to his care. At such times there will always be a choice. Being your husband's 'ezer' will enable you to make that godly choice, preventing resentment, anger, jealousy and discontent-ment from setting in.

We will be able to face this challenge only if our own faith in God's goodness is strong, and if we have been regularly preaching biblical truth to ourselves. Like Mary, sitting in a position of learning at the Master's feet, we are to be thinking theologians, extending ourselves in biblical knowledge and wisdom. We are to be women who have 'chosen what is better' (Luke 10:42) and have drawn deeply from the well of grace and spiritual insight, so that we are able to minister to our husbands and those whom the Lord has entrusted to us.

Our relationship with the Lord is *the* most important thing in our lives because . . .

f. It will prepare us for the day of trouble
Whether or not we have thus far in life experienced it, Psalm 27:5 ('In the day of trouble he will keep me safe in his dwelling') assures us that the day of trouble will come to each of us in one form or another. It may be a sudden phone call, a dreaded verdict from the consultant, a family crisis. Maybe it will be the shattered dream of childlessness. Maybe it will be when that young adult, whom you had sought to nurture in the things of God, turns his back on these precious gifts. Maybe it will be when a church fellowship has its heart split open through division.

But come it surely will. And at that crisis moment every sermon you have ever heard, every hour you have ever spent with the Lord and his Word will have been preparation for such a time. How you deal with that news will expose what your faith is truly based upon. Only if we have experienced the Lord's daily presence in our life will spiritual wisdom and faith allow us to 'trace the rainbow through the rain'[10] and trust God's sovereign and loving will.

During 2009, a minister and his wife from Cuckfield, Phil and Rosie Crowter, faced their own day of trouble. Through a series of emails to their praying friends, they traced their personal journey through Phil's fight with cancer. Here, with

Rosie's permission, is an extract from one of Phil's emails written just weeks before he died. The email was headed: 'Even though I walk through the valley of the shadow of death'.

> The consultant confirmed this morning that there is no more sensible treatment, as the cancer is still growing despite the chemo. This was expected, and Rosie and I have been processing this news during the past fortnight. We know that the Lord can miraculously intervene, but our expectation is for the Lord to take me home. That sounds all very peaceful (and a wonderful blessing), but death is a monster and the process is very painful for Rosie and the family . . . Please pray that somehow the Lord will make these final days fruitful ones, that he will be increasingly precious, and heaven a joy to anticipate. Pray that we all will cling to him to the end, trusting that he is love and only has good plans for his children.

Their experience was not triumphalistic, but it was real and deep, born out of a relationship with their Saviour, where faith and trust in God's almighty purposes had been grown and nurtured over the years. And it is only our constant relationship with the Saviour that will prepare us for the day of trouble when it arrives.

Our relationship with the Lord is *the* most important thing in our lives because . . .

g. It will empower us joyfully to serve others
It is impossible for us to give to others what we have not already received ourselves. We cannot genuinely impart gospel truths and experience that we have not personally received from the Lord. Without the motivation of grace, Christian

service will eventually exhaust and sap us because we will be serving in our own strength and not the strength of the Lord.

If we are doing ministry in our own strength, glorifying ourselves, it will ultimately enslave us and become a joyless burden. Luke's Gospel records the story of the two sisters, Martha and Mary. While Mary sat at Jesus' feet receiving from him, Martha bustled about in the kitchen feeling resentful. She had a ministry, but the spirit she brought to it was all wrong because she had not received from Jesus. Some ministers' wives I have known have come eventually to resent their ministries, just like Martha. It was the ministry itself rather than Christ that they were serving.

In this regard, one of the most liberating things the Lord has shown me recently, as we serve both the church family and those as yet unsaved, is to define clearly the things we can do, the things we can't do and the things that only the Holy Spirit can do.

The things we can – indeed must – do are love, care, support, show compassion, encourage, advise, warn, and model godly living within our sphere of influence, both in the church and beyond.

However, there are many things that we just can't do. We can't lead other people's lives for them, can't alter the backgrounds that have shaped their lives, can't discipline their children for them, can't make them become Christians, can't put the desire in their hearts to come to the prayer meeting or make peripheral church attenders become more involved in the life of the church. Only the Holy Spirit will be able to bring dead hearts to life, heal broken backgrounds and motivate people to seek and serve him.

So often I've felt impatient with people who have ignored sound godly advice or who have not been as committed to the church as I think they should be. However, understanding the clear distinctions between what I can and can't do and what only the Holy Spirit can do has enabled me to serve God's people with a much greater freedom and love.

Our relationship with the Lord is *the* most important thing in our lives because . . .

h. It will enable us to persevere and finish strong

'In the Christian life it's not how you start that matters. It's how you finish'.[11] And only an ongoing, ever-deepening relationship with the Lord will enable us to finish strong, despite all of Satan's ambushes on the road of life. Over the years Satan will incessantly do all in his power to knock us off course by distraction, disappointment and disobedience.

Finishing well will mean that we are walking with God personally at the end of our lives. Statistics and anecdotal evidence are stark reminders to us all that we are to make no assumptions that we will automatically finish strong in our relationship with the Lord. It is only our ongoing walk with the Saviour that will sustain us till the end.

Indeed, as the years pass and we travel along the Christian way, the Lord may well start to withdraw certain ministries and loved ones from us. Work that we initiated many years ago, and in which we have served faithfully week by week, will be entrusted to younger, more able women, and we will need the Spirit to give us grace to pass the baton on to them. We are constantly to remind ourselves that we are about the Lord's work – not about making a name for ourselves.

God may take us from our church family that we have loved and served with a passion. Again we are to remind ourselves that there will undoubtedly come a time when people attending the church which you and your husband have so treasured will never even have heard of you! Yet the church of God will continue to march on until the day of Christ's return.

We should always remember that the Lord may one day take our husbands from us too, and there will be no hectic family life, no busy church programme, no partner to rely upon. All that will remain will be our relationship with the Lord and his sustaining power.

Mark Ashton had enjoyed many years of fruitful ministry at St Andrew the Great in Cambridge. But a diagnosis of cancer brought it home clearly to him that he was unlikely to live to see his retirement. Just before the Lord called him into his presence at Easter 2010, Mark wrote these moving words:

> My death may be the event with which my physical life on earth ends, but it will also be the moment at which my relationship with Jesus becomes complete. That relationship is the only thing that has made sense of my physical life, and at my death it will be everything.

What an honour to know people like Mark who have had their ministries, their church family, their loved one taken from them, yet continue to rejoice in the Saviour whom they have loved and served down through the decades. They have fought the good fight, they have run the race, they have kept the faith. They press on to the prize, which is Christ, and they anticipate the crown of righteousness. They will receive the greatest accolade of all that can be given: 'Well done, good and faithful servant!' (Matthew 25:23).

In closing this foundational chapter, we need to recognize the reality that, while we all give mental assent to these truths, in reality we often find it difficult to nurture our love for, and relationship with, the Lord. Let's ask ourselves the question:

Why then do we find it so hard to nurture this relationship with the Lord?

- We have not truly understood the implications of **grace**. OK, we are happy to admit that it was all of God's grace when we became Christians, but as we go on in our Christian lives we still somehow subconsciously believe that God's blessing on our lives is conditional upon our activity and performance for him. We fail to remember that it was grace that saved us, it is grace that keeps us and grace that will bring us to glory. It would be well worth looking into our hearts once again and asking God to reveal the precious liberating truth of the glorious gospel of grace.
- We have forgotten that the Christian life is essentially lived by **faith**. It is all about an unseen realm, hidden treasures and future glory. We cannot physically measure the depth of our relationship with God, whereas our physical service for the King is very tangible, very visible and very obvious for all to see.

The Christian writer, Hannah More, comments that 'the things of time, being near seem great and so hide from our view the things of eternity'.[12] We constantly need to be bringing the things that are eternal and hidden into the focus of our daily consciousness and thoughts. We need to have hearts which are seeking after God, so that our minds are renewed daily, so that we begin to 'think God's thoughts after him' and have his eternal world ever before our eyes.

- We have failed to recognize that we battle against the **world**, the **flesh** and the **devil**. The sin that still dwells within us has no interest whatsoever in humbly listening to God's Word, and neither does Satan. It is amazing how many things come to our minds just as we are about to sit down and spend time alone with God. So many distractions, so many diversions – everything conspires against us sitting at the Master's feet.

- We have not taken into account that there are very definite '**seasons**' of life. Each one has its own blessings and opportunities, but each also has its own temptations and difficulties. And I particularly want to encourage every young mum who reads this book with this assurance: while everything in your family life at the moment seemingly makes it impossible for you to have any routine or quality time with the Lord, things definitely will get easier, and there will come a day when you will have much more time to read the Bible and meditate on the Lord.

During the years when we were raising our four young children, my spiritual life was an absolute shambles, and I would have been thoroughly ashamed to admit the paucity of my relationship with the Lord. But thank God again, it's all about his grace – not my performance. So I encourage you to take heart and remember that he doesn't ask: 'How long is your quiet time?', but rather, 'Daughter, do you love me?'

As you read this book I pray that you will sense that your greatest calling, far beyond that of being a busy minister's wife or servant of the local church, is that of knowing the inestimable joy of being united with Christ through his work on the cross and being in a relationship with him that enables you to serve him out of a heart that truly loves him.

For further reflection or action

1. Why is a close walk with Jesus Christ of paramount importance for a minister's wife?
2. Is reading God's Word a delight to you? Think of ways in which you can, even with limited time, enjoy the Bible and meditate on it so that it shapes your character and life.
3. When have you found that getting closer to Jesus was not a cosy or comfortable experience? How has God used that in your life? Are there some idols which have been exposed and which need to be repeatedly expelled?
4. Take time now to think about the love of God for you in Jesus Christ, and to answer the foundational question: 'Daughter, do you love me?'

2. Her responsibility to her husband: A suitable helper

by Kath Paterson

Kath grew up in London with parents who loved and lived God's Word and was converted on the eve of her eleventh birthday. When the 'new minister' came to Trinity Road Chapel in Tooting, little did she realize that the 'boy' she was going to marry had arrived with him!

Kath married Andy Paterson in 1979 knowing that he felt called to full-time ministry. Andy became lay pastor of Summerstown Mission in Tooting, and during the five years that followed Kath relinquished her secretarial work to concentrate on looking after their two young children. A move from SW to SE London found them at The Slade in Plumstead where Andy became assistant minister. In 1988 the family moved to Bristol where Andy took up the pastorate of Kensington Baptist Church. Opportunities opened up for Kath to develop a ministry among women, including other ministry wives, and today she is involved in conference planning and also speaks at women's events.

She has had many opportunities to join Andy in visiting overseas workers 'in situ', giving her greater insight into the challenges of cross-cultural mission. In January 2012 Andy and Kath hope to complete twenty-four years of intensive yet joyful ministry among the church family at KBC when Andy becomes Director of Mission for the FIEC. Kath welcomes the opportunity to develop supportive links with many ministry wives.

Kath remains heavily involved in literacy work through the Easton Jubilee Trust, a charity working to support refugees in the inner city, and she is also a governor at a local primary school. She enjoys music, gardening and Zumba!

It was Sunday morning and, just as on any other Sunday, the minister's red car was whizzing down the hill like one of the Red Arrows before negotiating the narrow streets of the inner city below. However, all was not well. While the kids in the back were caught up in their own banter, an atmosphere was gathering momentum in the front. The car finally came to a standstill in a side road opposite the church, and while the kids raced off to find their friends, the minister and his unexploded bomb were left sitting in the front seats.

Call it what you like: the moody blues, pity-party extravaganza or PMT, but she railed on about how miserable *she* was feeling and how *she* didn't think *she* could manage a plastic smile that morning. But no sooner had those words slipped off her tongue than she knew it! Now she'd really overstepped the mark.

He was very direct. He needed to be. He said he was sorry that she was struggling so much, but *he* had a service to lead and a sermon to preach. If she wanted to hide away in the back row that was fine, but he had a congregation to face. He wasn't cross with her. (Her conscience would have found it more tolerable if he had been.) No, something more serious was happening. Her negative state of mind was beginning to affect him.

Now you might be thinking that this was rather harsh treatment, but I have to disagree and tell you that the man I married is incredibly understanding and supportive. Rather, to my shame I can vividly remember how I'd indulged myself that morning with a huge dollop of self-pity and let him have it at a completely inappropriate moment, rather than taking myself in hand and exercising self-control – even though I was really struggling that day. I remember the shame I felt as I got out of the car. I knew that I had let the Lord down as well as my husband. I realized just how close I had come to jeopard-izing my husband's ministry that morning! My self-centred emotions had been transferred on to his shoulders . . . because I knew only too well that whenever I struggled it affected him too.

But I can thank God for important lessons learned that day: lessons about myself and the importance of guarding my heart. And a stark reminder about the awesome respon-sibility and privilege God has given me to encourage my husband in his ministry – and not just on a Sunday morning either!

As a ministry wife this means I will endeavour to be ready and willing to show my support as he seeks faithfully to teach the Bible and lead the community of God's people he's been entrusted with. Therefore I will make it my aim to encourage him all I can, even if this means at times that I will need to button my lip.

It doesn't mean I can't be real. That would make a complete mockery of the intimate relationship God has given us to enjoy together. But it does mean I will ask God's help in making me more vigilant against the devices of the enemy who attempts to use me to disarm my husband in the immense task God has set him apart to do.

So with this in mind, I will aim to:

Be his helper (according to God's design)

After God had made Adam out of the dust of the earth, he said, 'It is not good for the man to be alone. I will make a helper suitable for him' (Genesis 2:18). So God put Adam into a deep sleep, and reaching into his side he created the perfect companion for him. She would be his closest friend and would complement and bless him in every area of his life. Together reflecting the harmonious relationship of the Godhead, they were to set about working to fulfil the creation mandate God had given them.

In the New Testament we read that 'neither was man created for woman, but woman for man' (1 Corinthians 11:9). Eve was created for Adam and not the other way round. But as his helper, Eve certainly wasn't inferior to Adam. She was an intimate part of him. Adam had been created from the dust – but Eve had come from his very own body! Her status was equal to that of her husband, but her Creator's intention was that she would be different in the way she functioned within that special relationship. It is not for us therefore to stick out our chin and voice our objection. When God in his infinite wisdom decided the role Eve would assume, a role that would complement Adam's, there were no trousers to be seen anywhere.

How foolish we are therefore if we allow our hearts to become hardened. In Exodus 4 we read about Zipporah, wife of Moses. She did not see eye-to-eye with her husband over the circumcision of their sons. In fact she was so defiantly opposed towards God's plan for her husband that it nearly cost him his life and ministry.

In God's all-wise and loving way he has created each one of us to be the helper that our husbands need. We can be greatly encouraged knowing that we have been created with the *ability* to fulfil that purpose within our marriage, and furthermore the Bible gives us clear guidelines on how we should be living as Christian wives. Ephesians 5:24 reminds me that I must submit to my husband in everything, complementing him as we work together at our marriage, and serve alongside him within that relationship. So whether I'm married to a mechanic, a master-chef or a minister, I must submit to my husband as the church submits to Christ. We've already seen the importance of a close daily walk with Jesus. That is our number-one priority. Everything else about us, who we are and what we do, flows from this. It is only as we seek to live in joyful submission to God, fulfilling the tasks and responsibilities he has entrusted to us, that we can obey him by joyfully submitting to our husbands. And as a minister's wife there are particular ways in which I can show that submission as I love and support my husband.

Be his wife (he is your husband before he is a minister)

Paul outlines the job description of a minister in a nutshell: 'to prepare God's people for works of service, so that the body of Christ may be built up' (Ephesians 4:12). This is a huge privilege, but one that also carries an awesome responsibility. It will bring particular times of sorrow and pain because it will involve working alongside people with broken lives – people like you and me – and that can be messy. But the joys far outweigh the sorrows as our faithful God goes on transforming lives by his grace. How vital therefore that a minister receives the support and encouragement of a 'suitable helper'. And if God has called our husbands and equipped them for the task of building up the body of believers entrusted to them, so as wives we can be confident that God will also give us the grace to support them in their important task.

We know little about the prophet Ezekiel's wife. But we do know that, despite the outrageous things God required of her husband as he acted out God's message before the exiles, she remained the 'delight of [her husband's] eyes' (Ezekiel 24:16).

Maybe you are anxious or concerned because you don't think you have what it takes to be a minister's wife, and you certainly don't have the 'skills' that you perceive other ministers' wives as having.

What if that is the case? Are these skills and abilities the *essentials*? I would like to suggest not! The most practical and godly way for a wife to support her husband actually involves *being* more than *doing*. Your gifts might not be in music, running 'Mums & Tots' or baking cakes! What a relief, because that is not the issue! The point is that your husband's life is more than just about ministry (as hard as some of us might find that to believe). First and foremost he is your husband *before* he is a minister! And therefore the best way you can support him is by *being there* for him. By being his best friend and lover, his prayer partner and number-one encourager. By being ready to listen, being loyal and trustworthy, and by being wise in building a refuge for him – that's what I would call *being* a minister's wife. (All of these things will be unpacked later.) And while there are some issues that relate particularly to the ministry marriage, we are called to live as examples to the women in our churches in all of the above areas.

Be his best friend and lover

When Paul wrote to Titus, he had a twofold purpose for instructing him in how to teach the older women. These women were to live godly lives that would qualify them to teach the younger women in the church. And in Titus 2:4 we find that the first seminar for these young women was called 'How to love your husband'. Paul uses the word *phileo*, meaning 'love that cherishes'. This deep-friendship love is certainly ignited by the first spark of romance, but it is also a love that must be developed and practised throughout the whole of married life. Your husband should be your best friend, and you should treasure his love and friendship above any other.

So do we really need to be *taught* how to love him? Isn't love something that comes naturally? But surely the continual rise in marriage breakdown and divorce proves without doubt that this kind of love requires nurture and hard work. Are we continuing to honour our husband with that coveted 'best-friend' status, or have we stolen the privilege from him and given it to someone else? When you hear some exciting news that you can't wait to pass on or find yourself in need of a listening ear, is your husband the first person to whom you turn, or are you more likely to phone your mum or one of your children or a close friend?

Are you communicating freely and openly with him, making every opportunity for your unique friendship to grow? Developing such an intimate relationship must be a lifelong top priority. It won't just happen. It takes hard work and commitment.

So how can we continue to keep the fires of love and friendship red-hot?

- Tell him you love him – and keep doing this every day for the rest of your life!

- Let your children see how much you love their dad
- Honour him
- Forgive him
- Be proud of him
- Smile at him
- Listen to your husband without criticism as he shares visions and dreams
- Thank him often and show appreciation, and not just when you're alone together
- Don't complain when things are tough
- Allow him his space – he needs it
- Keep romantic love alight
- Discover his number-one 'love language', in other words, the optimum way in which he will know that you love him[1]
- Plan a regular date night. Chill out, have fun and laugh together! Take it in turns to plan and surprise each other. Be creative. This does not have to involve big spending, but why not save up for a special night out just once in a while?
- And if you have just skipped over the previous point because you are too busy – then you really *are* too busy!
- Schedule a regular time to talk through issues that concern you as a couple – but definitely not church matters!
- And last but certainly not least, make love to him . . . often

At the end of C. J. Mahaney's book *Sex, Romance, and the Glory of God*,[2] C. J.'s wife Carolyn talks frankly to wives and begins by sharing a memory:

> Several years ago at a church leadership conference, I hosted a panel of ministers' wives at a women's session. We fielded questions on a wide variety of topics – from childrearing to

counselling women in crisis situations. Then a woman from the audience posed the question: 'What is one thing you have learned that encourages your husband the most?' As the other women on the panel answered, I pondered my response. I knew what C. J.'s answer would be, but dare I say that? And then it was my turn. 'Make love to him,' I blurted out. 'That's what my husband would say if he were here!' The room erupted into a wave of nervous, knowing laughter . . .

And I have to agree with Carolyn's brave response, and unashamedly confirm that my husband would say the same – and so probably too would yours! But what is *our* response to that?

When Adam first clapped eyes on Eve, an exciting new emotion would have sprung to life from within him. His Creator had equipped him with the 'wiring' for this emotion, but the power only got switched on when he saw this awesome creature God had brought to him as his wife, standing there in all her radiant beauty. I'm sure his first thought was not: 'Great! I'll get her to work straight away in the garden.'

As part of this exclusive and intimate relationship, God gave the awesome gift of sex for the man and his wife to enjoy together as 'one flesh'. His purpose was for them to enjoy the security of physical and emotional oneness as they shared together the most intimate pleasure on earth!

Paul puts the place of sex within marriage in the context of the pure and sacrificial love Christ has for his church (Ephesians 5:31–32). And there can be no higher love than that! This kind of selfless giving of one to the other brings a unity that can only come from such unconditional love and acceptance. But when sin entered the world, discontentment and selfishness also sprang to life. And any part of a marriage relationship can be spoiled through discontentment and selfishness. In sex this is seen when one partner places his or her own needs or desires above those of the other. Let me ask you: are you placing the needs of your husband above your own, or has your desire for sex begun to wane?

Paul could not have been more explicit in reminding us in 1 Corinthians 7:3–5 that it is a wife's responsibility to give her body willingly to her husband. And her husband similarly has to make an effort to satisfy his wife sexually. The reason is clear (in verse 5) and also comes to us as a sombre warning: 'so that Satan will not tempt you because of your lack of self-control'. Sexual enjoyment within marriage is part of God's good intention to protect us from temptation to sinful lust. I don't need to make or labour the point that breakdowns in ministry marriages are continually on the increase, and often as a result of sexual temptation *inside* the church.

But I must be real. There are times when we all find ourselves on a treadmill – and I don't mean at the local gym! We are trudging along with responsibilities of all shapes and sizes balanced on our shoulders, and before we know it we find ourselves under that familiar blanket of perpetual tiredness. Tiredness is the number-one passion extinguisher. In the real world there will be times when acute tiredness is unavoidable. Therefore we can only determine personally, and with our husband, to make what changes we can to alleviate some of that tiredness. It might mean thinking and acting creatively to make sex happen. But make the changes we must.

Part of God's judgment on Eve was that her desire would be for her husband. That sounds wonderful. But God did not mean a lovey-dovey desire. Far from it. She was now going to discover that she had sinful, selfish motives that would make her desire to control and dominate her husband to suit her own agenda.

So what about the times when we could rightfully be accused of placing obstacles in the path of our husband's desire? We certainly need to repent of the selfish attitude that frequently puts our own needs and emotions first. We need to examine our own motives and desires, and this might mean reorganizing time and priorities.

Ask God to renew or increase your passion for the man he's given *to you* so that you become bolder in the way you express your physical love, and delight and bless him with the joy of frequent and regular sexual intimacy.

Be his prayer partner

When Paul wrote to Timothy (1 Timothy 3:1–7), he listed the essential character qualities for an elder or minister/teacher. The man, he said, must be blameless, a faithful husband, temperate, self-controlled, respectable, hospitable, able to teach, not a drunkard, not violent or greedy for money, but gentle, and not quarrelsome or covetous. He must also be able to manage his family well and have a good reputation with outsiders. Some list!

If we want to support our husbands in the most effective possible way, there will be no substitute for prayer. Paul regularly stressed the importance of prayer as he encouraged the believers in the first century. And his prayers continue to encourage *us* as we serve God in the twenty-first century, especially as we pray that these godly desires will be seen more and more in our husbands' lives and ministries:

And this is my prayer: that your love may abound more and more in knowledge and depth of insight, so that you may be able to discern what is best and may be pure and blameless until the day of Christ, filled with the fruit of righteousness that comes through Jesus Christ – to the glory and praise of God. (Philippians 1:9–11)

We are now living in a generation where more and more ministry wives are involved in full- or part-time work outside the home. Others need to focus on the important work of caring for young children or elderly relatives. Perhaps few are in a position to serve more widely among their church family and local community. But whatever the day-to-day situation, beware of a preoccupation with a busy schedule which continually dictates the next demand. The result will be that prayer concentrates solely on the immediate or the urgent. Prayer can so easily become impersonal, adopting the lazy pattern of asking God to 'bless' this person or that situation, rather than praying in a specific and informed way. But if we want to stand alongside our husbands by praying effectively for them, then we cannot be content with such a limited prayer life. A wife knows her husband best of all, better than the church members know him, or might like to think they know him.

Several years ago I came across a small book of prayers compiled by Stormie Omartian to complement her book, *The Power of a Praying Wife*.[3] It encouraged me to pray beyond the immediate and the urgent and systematically to bring before the Lord every area of my husband's life and character: to pray for his growth in grace, and for holiness in his life and character; that he would know wisdom in priorities and decision-making; for his faithful handling of God's Word and for Holy Spirit power as he taught and preached; for physical, spiritual and emotional protection; for him in his role as a husband to me, and father to our now grown-up children; for integrity and humility in his interaction with others, and for self-control and faithfulness when he was shut away in his study where no human eye could see him.

Do you pray that your husband's *life* will be fruitful, and that he would know ongoing Holy Spirit help as he seeks to be obedient to God (1 Timothy 3:2)? Do you pray that he will point to Jesus by the way he lives privately behind closed doors as well as in front of others, whether they be believers or unbelievers? Paul told the Christians in Ephesus that he was praying these things into their lives:

> I have not stopped giving thanks for you, remembering you in my prayers. I keep asking that the God of our Lord Jesus Christ, the glorious Father, may give you the Spirit of wisdom and revelation, so that you may know him better.
> (Ephesians 1:16–17)

There are many times when I am the only person who is aware of a particular situation that my husband is facing. I realize that sometimes I am the only one who fully understands the extent of the pressure he is under and how that pressure is affecting him. Over the years I have come to learn about his strengths as well as his weaknesses. I see when he's physically tired and pick up when he is struggling emotionally. Sometimes I overhear a difficult or sensitive phone conversation, and that gives me an opportunity to pray that he will be given compassion, humility and wisdom in how he responds. Sometimes he shares with me a difficult email that needs a wise and considered reply – and yet again I can pray.

Do you share together the priorities, responsibilities and tasks facing you each day? Do you make it a priority to ask your husband how you can pray for him *today*? Are you aware when he is preparing for Sunday's ministry? If there is any time when we should be praying, this is surely the time. Ask the Holy Spirit to help him understand and apply God's Word faithfully as he prepares, and pray for boldness and courage for him to preach what God has laid on his heart – irrespective of what others might think or say. Paul requested the Ephesian church to pray this way: 'Pray also for me, that whenever I open my mouth, words may be given me so that I will fearlessly make known the mystery of the gospel . . . Pray that I may declare it fearlessly, as I should' (Ephesians 6:19–20).

But over the years as we have been involved in ministry, I have also become increasingly aware of something I can't relate to. Although I've learned to appreciate and understand the nature of my husband's ministry, I will never *fully* know the immense burden of responsibility that falls on his shoulders as a minister – and part of that involves the loneliness of leadership! Paul concludes his long list of sufferings (2 Corinthians 11:28) by saying that 'Besides everything else, *I* face daily the pressure of *my* concern for all the churches' (italics mine).

And so I need to go on praying for grace to be more faithful in taking hold of the opportunities that I am given to pray for my husband, realizing at the same time how much the Lord needs to go on refining and changing his wife.

Be his encourager

Proverbs 3:27 tells us 'not [to] withhold good from those to whom it is due, when it is in your power to do it' (ESV). Wives have a far greater opportunity than the most loyal and supportive church member to do *good* to their husbands by encouragement.

Encouragement by words

All our words carry power either to build up or to destroy. There is no middle ground. Sometimes wisdom will show us that it is kinder to exercise self-control and hold back from saying something that could discourage. But this involves a choice and means that we need to think before we open our mouths. I have never forgotten a sermon application my husband borrowed from Alan Redpath: using 't-h-i-n-k' as an acrostic challenges me to consider whether my words are 'true – helpful – inspiring – necessary – kind' before I open my mouth. How many times have I engaged my brain *after* I have opened my mouth? Then I realized that what I had said to my husband would have been better kept to myself because it was neither helpful nor kind – and it was certainly unnecessary.

My husband knows I am his biggest critic, but that doesn't mean that everything I say is negative. His most vulnerable time is without doubt after he's given his all in preaching.

Bruce Thielemann, the gifted Presbyterian preacher of almost a generation ago, said: 'To preach, to really preach, is to die naked a little at a time, and to know each time you do it that you must do it again.'[4]

Now do you see how important it is for a wife to say something positive and encouraging as soon as possible after her husband has preached? Even though preaching is not about the preacher, the very nature of what he is doing can leave him vulnerable and susceptible to doubt, if not to pride. No preacher can say that negative comments will just go over his head. However long a man has been in ministry, negative criticism still has the potential to wound. And conversely, the same can be said about positive affirmation and the danger of self-sufficiency and pride.

You will be aware of the kind of week your husband has just had and if unexpected demands have whittled down his time for sermon preparation. So be real in your encouragement and remind him of these things. Encouragement does not mean that we blatantly lie through our teeth and tell our husband that his preaching was amazing when it wasn't. We must be real, without flattering with empty platitudes. Solomon didn't mince his words when he said,

A lying tongue hates those it hurts,
   and a flattering mouth works ruin.
(Proverbs 26:28)

But there *is* a place for constructive criticism. I am not referring
to the nit-picking of self-righteously pointing out a gram-
matical blunder he made, rather those times when we can
constructively help by pointing out a mannerism or habit that
is in danger of becoming a hindrance.

In the early years of ministry, if my husband used a phrase
or cliché well past its sell-by date or developed a mannerism
that had begun to grate on me, then I assumed it was probably
having the same effect on others. This didn't happen often,
but when it did *I* wanted to be the one to tell him. You see, I
learned about this the hard way! Someone eager to do my
husband a kindness came to our home to tell him about a
minor irritation that spoiled his preaching for him. I remember
my husband being very gracious in his response. However, I
was gutted because I realized that this person had a valid point,
and if only I had spoken up I could have avoided this embarrassing situation. But there's also an appropriate time to raise
an issue – and that is never on a Sunday. Look for an opportunity
later in the week, and guard your heart before you open your
mouth. Being over-zealous about dishing out criticism in an
effort to help can result in damaging confidence and lead
to discouragement.

Encouragement by listening

Listening is so much more than just hearing what someone
else says. We listen and respond every day to greetings,
requests, instructions, information and much more. Some
responses are necessarily automatic, but there will be those
times when our husbands need to share at a deeper level, and

it is vital that we engage with them by listening intently: not just listening with our ears because we're in the same room, but showing that we are fully engaged. And that might mean turning off the iron so we can give eye contact, or pausing during a meal rather than taking that next mouthful. Breaking off from what we are doing is showing without words that we value and honour our husband and what he wants to share. But maybe that is not the hardest part! It also means we will show control about when we speak, rather than constantly interrupting with our own questioning thoughts and opinions. That is something we need to go on learning.

Encouragement by reminders

Years ago when I was working as a secretary in a London hospital, part of my responsibility was to remind my boss of things that might have slipped his mind. This didn't mean he was incompetent, for he certainly was not, but he did have many pressures and demands on his time. In a similar way I will try to remind my husband of things people may have shared with one or other of us, things that we can follow up by means of an encouraging inquiry. I do not accuse him of being uncaring if he needs reminding. He may have remembered yesterday, but today (especially if it's a Sunday) his mind is focused on the greater task. We model grace when we remember that even the smallest details that might seem insignificant to us might be massive in someone else's life.

Be a loyal friend

Ministry life is life to some extent in the public eye. People both inside and outside the church observe what we say and how we say it. They watch the way we live and take note of our reactions to the experiences that come our way.

Honouring the covenant that we made on our wedding day means ongoing loyalty in the marriage partnership. In addition, 1 Timothy 3:2 tells us that the 'overseer' is to live wisely, carefully and above reproach, and since the ministry couple are 'one flesh', that means the wife too. It is therefore vital that we are seen and heard at all times to be a loyal supporter of our husband. We should never say anything negative about him or anything that could be construed as negative, and always be ready to affirm him where appropriate. I am only too aware of the times when my husband gets it wrong. But I am no different. Therefore out of loyalty and in humility, I'll make it my aim never to argue with him or put him down in front of others – including my children. And for those of us privileged to be working as part of a ministry team, we must be just as vigilant in our loyalty towards our co-workers too.

Be his trustworthy confidante

You have to be trustworthy to enable him to share his heart. Your husband needs a safe and loving environment where he is not going to be misunderstood or criticized if he wants to express how he really feels. My husband also needs to know for sure that I am not going to tell *anyone* the things he has shared with me.

A large part of ministry is spent listening, and at times the ministry couple will find themselves confronted with the deepest and darkest secrets of a person's heart and life. Whether this information is shared with both of us or I hear it second-hand from my husband (and he always asks permission before sharing with me – and vice versa), he needs to know that I can be trusted not to go tripping off to bend someone else's ear – in the guise of 'just for your prayers'.

And we need wisdom in the way we respond. There may be occasions when it is clear that professional help is needed, and therefore before a person has opened their heart to us we need to avoid giving any assurance of confidentiality that could tie our hands. Vigilance serves not only for our own protection, but also for the good of the other person. Therefore be on your guard if someone opens a conversation by saying, 'Don't tell anyone else about this but . . .'

Be his refuge-provider

Skim the magazine rack of any supermarket and you are sure to find countless articles pushing the latest innovative ideas for making your home evermore coordinated and efficient. The fact that you would be living in a show house rather than a home does not kill the appeal. But browse the biblically sound, relevant books on a bookstall, and any title that challenges us to reorganize our lives on the home front is quickly bypassed. They definitely kill the appeal. Is this because we recoil from a retro image of ourselves in a frilly apron with matching duster on our head? I doubt it. I think it has more to do with getting our godly priorities skewed. The prudent words of Solomon tell us:

> The wise woman builds her house,
> but with her own hands the foolish one tears hers down.
> (Proverbs 14:1)

How we spend our working day will differ according to our priorities, but are we wisely investing enough hours in order to build a place of refuge for our family? We place a high priority on ministering grace into other people's lives, but how much do we minister grace to our husband when he walks through the door in order to relax in his own home? Only you know if he favours minimalist or muddle, but what kind of atmosphere is he likely to walk into? Do you keep up with his priorities so that he gets fed and watered on time, or is he greeted with another note on the freezer door to 'pop in a pizza'?! A well-run, orderly home is God-honouring, but our personal attitudes matter more.

As a ministry wife, your input through the ordinary and everyday minutiae of life is more crucial to gospel work than you could ever imagine.

For further reflection or action

1. In what ways can a woman jeopardize her husband's ministry?
2. Review the ways in which you can keep the fires of friendship and love within your marriage red-hot. What could you be working on right now?
3. Plan a date with your husband.
4. Take time to compose a prayer for your husband, bearing in mind the challenges and struggles he is facing at present.

3. Her responsibility to her family: What about the children?

by Ann Benton

Ann married John Benton at the age of twenty-one, when neither she nor he had any idea that John would spend the larger part of his working life in full-time Christian ministry. They are both from non-Christian backgrounds: John was converted at school and Ann at Sussex University, where they met in the 1960s. Ann graduated in psychology and trained and worked as a teacher in primary schools and special schools until the first of their four children was born. The family moved from Liverpool to Guildford, Surrey when John was called to the pastorate of Chertsey Street Baptist Church in 1980. John and Ann have lived and worked there ever since. For most of that time Ann has been fully employed but unwaged. She is aware that as such she is a disappearing species. The four 'children' are all now grown-up and married. Ann moved seamlessly from caring for children to caring for parents: her mother-in-law remains a major assignment to this day. Ann has written a number of books on family issues. Between family and church responsibilities, she also runs parenting courses and speaks at conferences. She delights to help at the local primary school on a voluntary basis, teaching singing and running the school choir. At one time she was Chairman of the London Women's Convention. She counts among her happiest times being in a kitchen with Delia Smith or on a sofa with Charles Dickens.

Some young couples set out on ministerial life unencumbered by dependants. They may or may not embrace the buy-one-get-one-free model of ministry, but they are able to throw themselves into church life and ministry without considering how that involvement may affect others. But the presence or arrival of children or needy elderly parents brings a whole new dimension to ministerial life.

Of course, in many ways it is also an attractive dimension. It evidences normality and a natural link and empathy with others in the church and community who are facing the challenges of parenthood or the care of elderly relatives. But some ministers' wives find that a disturbing tension ensues. What actually do we owe to our families? What are the implications of our ministry for our dependants? Is there a sense in which our children need to be protected from the church?

In seeking to answer those kinds of questions, I'd like to suggest the following:

1. That the responsibility of the minister's wife to her family is the same as that of any other Christian wife;
2. That there are particular temptations and issues attached to life in the manse or rectory;

3. That it is possible to embrace and enjoy the most demanding seasons of our lives.

The responsibility of the minister's wife to her family is the same as that of any other Christian wife

Paul's instructions about widows who were to be supported by the local church are contained in 1 Timothy 5. Through these instructions we learn something about how a Christian woman can please God. We learn that family needs are to be high up on the agenda. Caring for elderly parents is 'putting your religion into practice' (verse 4). It is not an option as such, nor is it to be played off against service in the church. Failure to care for your family is 'denying the faith' and makes you 'worse than an unbeliever' (verse 8).

So whatever the occupation of the man she married, a believing woman has to be diligent and unselfish in her family responsibilities. Her children and her parents have a legitimate claim on her time and her energy. A minister's wife might rightly consider that she must be well known for her good deeds, just as these widows in Timothy's church were, but note what is first on the list of the good deeds for which she must be famous (verse 10): it is the bringing up of children. So a woman who at a particular period in her life is more or less fully occupied in meeting the needs of her family is doing a good deed.

Motherhood is greatly undervalued in the twenty-first century. It is termed a 'career break', as though the career is the important thing and motherhood is something you can take a few weeks off to do. Later, after the briefest possible interval, you can resume the real work of your life. Not so in the Bible. Motherhood is eminently significant.

It is crucial to the handing on of essential truth (Proverbs 1:8); it is God's gift, a fact to bear in mind in an age when women think they control their own fertility (Genesis 25:21); it is vital to the raising of secure, happy and healthy children. A mother cannot be replaced by a childcare professional, because a child is not precious to a carer, however well qualified the latter may be, in the way that he or she is precious to a mother. That childcare professional will go home at the end of her shift to her own precious children. No-one else can do what a mother does for her children and even teenagers need mothers.

Perhaps *especially*, teenagers need mothers. Do not think that it is job done when your children enter secondary school. Do not think that because they grunt and disappear into their bedrooms that what you do is worthless. I commented recently to one of my grown-up sons that because I had spent so many years in the home, unwaged, my state pension would be minuscule. He said to me, 'Well, I was the beneficiary of that.' But frankly, his gratitude was not discernible during the monosyllabic years.

It is a strange world we live in: while contemporary Western culture does not value motherhood, it is at the same time extremely child-centred. One of the current side effects of the pressure on mothers to return to paid employment is that women feel that when they are at home they have to compensate for their frequent absences by giving their children very intense attention or large quantities of material things. Neither of these strategies is healthy or necessary. Meeting your children's needs does not mean making them the centre of your universe. It does not mean expending all your energy in ensuring that every minute of the day they are being educated or entertained.

But meeting your children's needs does mean that you will make sure they have a secure and loving home, where they know they are significant and special and where you are paying due attention to their intellectual, social, physical and spiritual development. It is worth keeping in mind that some of those needs can be superbly met within the larger family circle of the church. Remembering this may relieve some of the sense of tension you experience.

Whenever I write or speak about motherhood I get asked about fathers. In stressing the importance of motherhood I am not devaluing fatherhood or saying that fathers can walk away and leave it all to the mothers. That is certainly not biblical. But neither is it biblical to say that mothers and fathers are interchangeable. And in this book I am talking about mothers. I do not think it is essential that parents take an equal share in the hands-on aspect of parenting. It does not take two parents to put the children to bed on a daily basis, even though it might be fun sometimes to do it together. In this age of the 'new man', mothers have high expectations of their husbands in terms of childcare. Sometimes those expectations are neither necessary nor reasonable. May I suggest that instead of nursing resentment (resentment which the children will quickly pick up on) that you are the one who is always changing the nappies, doing the school run, making the packed lunches, you look on this as a loving contribution which releases your husband into ministry. If he is the major wage-earner he is already making a contribution. I write this not to let fathers off the hook, but to warn women against allowing a root of bitterness to grow up. There may be times when you need to remind your husband of how much you value and need his help and input, but there is also a place for sacrifice, cheerfulness, fortitude and grace. Motherhood is something you do for God.

There are many books about how to do motherhood better, but at this point I want to encourage any mother who reads this not to be afraid to enjoy her children and the challenge of raising them. Relax! You can do this.

Meeting the needs of elderly and frail parents is generally a less attractive assignment, not least because this tends to crop up at a time when you have your hands pretty full with other things. Newspaper reports refer to the 'sandwich generation': middle-aged people who are looking after their children/ grandchildren in addition to their aged parents. But the Bible is quite clear about what we owe our parents. It is a debt that must be repaid to those who brought us up (1 Timothy 5:4). Matthew Henry comments that the fifth commandment includes: 'endeavouring, in everything, to be the comfort of their parents, and to make their old age easy to them'.[1] For some of us that will mean daily, hands-on care and attention; for others it might mean the daily phone call or the weekly visit. Some of the practical care and attention may be delegated to others, but whatever you decide in all good conscience before God to do for your parents, the salient point is that their happiness and comfort in old age is your concern. You cannot ignore their needs in the name of Christian service. Jesus himself was very clear on this point (Matthew 15:4–6).

There are particular temptations and issues attached to life in the manse or rectory

I first found out that motherhood as the wife of a teacher was different from motherhood as the wife of a minister in the summer of 1980. John and I had just begun in Guildford and were occupying the manse along with our two little boys aged two and four. Times have changed. In the twenty-first century people tend to dress down for church, but in the mid-to-late-twentieth century there was a tradition of Sunday best, which in some churches meant very formal attire. As a young and new minister's wife I always dressed my boys for church quite sweetly and smartly in their best T-shirts and dungarees. So I was intrigued to discover on my doorstep within a few weeks of John's induction a parcel containing two little white shirts. The sender was anonymous. It was a kind gift and I received it in that spirit. But it was also a comment. And it dawned on me then that there was now a whole new dimension to the raising of my children. Would the nameless giver have done the same for any other new family in the church? I think not. So for a minister's wife the principles of parenting remain the same, but the expectations of other people are different, and those expectations can significantly impact on your mothering.

In exploring this theme let us first consider three pitfalls to avoid. I will use fictional and literary examples to illustrate my points. But I stress that the temptation to go one or all three of these routes is at times strong. I have recognized this in myself and I have seen it in other ministers' wives too. These routes are neither beneficial to our children nor glorifying to God.

Telescopic philanthropy

In Charles Dickens' *Bleak House* there is a character called Mrs Jellyby. Dickens' masterful parables are packed with caricatures of human weakness. Dickens was no admirer of evangelicals, and perhaps his choice of name for this character, Mrs Jellyby, is a clue to where in the world this weakness was most likely to be found. The woman in question was not a minister's wife, but when we meet her in the novel it is as a mother of many young children and a person of remarkable dedication and strength of character. Mrs Jellyby devotes herself to a variety of good causes, in particular to the African project in Borrioboola-Gha. The progress of this project and the welfare of the orphans of Borrioboola-Gha is Mrs Jellyby's burning passion. No doubt she does a lot of good in Borrioboola-Gha. But meanwhile her children are literally tumbling down the stairs; they are woefully neglected both physically and emotionally, but their mother fails to see it. As Dickens eloquently puts it, 'Her eyes could see nothing nearer than Africa.'

Nothing nearer than Africa, or for a minister's wife nothing nearer than the church: that is *our* kind of telescopic philanthropy. As the wife of a church leader, you will want to support your husband in his work. Perhaps he needs all the support he can get, because the Lord has placed you in a small church with few committed and able-bodied members. You and your husband pray together for the church; you share a large vision; you see the work that needs to be done or that could be done and you see that the labourers are few and ill-equipped; you want to set an example in enthusiastic, undaunted service. So you roll your sleeves up and get stuck in. This becomes the project into which you pour your energy and you are doing it all for Jesus – taking a meal here, looking after someone else's children there, offering hospitality, visiting, delivering leaflets, preparing Sunday school, running the youth work or the women's meeting. And your children learn to get along with just a small fraction of your exhausted attention. You are seeing nothing nearer than the church, while metaphorically your children are tumbling down the stairs. None of us intends for this to happen, but sometimes it just does and it is scary.

One minister's wife told me of the time when she was making a lasagne for a family in the church who had just had a new baby. Her children came in from school and were delighted at the smell of home cooking, and she felt ashamed to admit to them that the lasagne was for others; she had not quite worked out what they themselves would be eating. As she took this delicious home-cooked meal to the needy family, that minister's wife realized that the trouble she had taken was not about service, but about pride and showing off what a good cook she was. Next time she had a similar mission she ordered the needy family a pizza, which didn't make her look like MasterChef, but still met their needs. And she made sure that her own children had a tasty home-cooked meal. Our children are also our ministry. Whatever your skills and gifts, don't expend them only outside the home. Let your family be the first beneficiaries.

Down with telescopic philanthropy! It leads to angry children, insecure children, and even unruly children.

The external focus

Another character from *Bleak House* is Mrs Pardiggle. Mrs Pardiggle does not entirely approve of Mrs Jellyby. She says,

> I do not go with Mrs Jellyby in her treatment of her young family. It has been noticed. It has been observed that her young family are excluded from participation in the objects to which she is devoted. She may be right, she may be wrong; but right or wrong, this is not my course with my young family. I take them everywhere.

So this is Mrs Pardiggle's idea: instead of telescopic philanthropy, take your children with you into the work. Enrol them! Involve them! Mrs Pardiggle gets her children up all year round in the very early morning to attend matins. And from there they accompany her on her daily round of visiting the poor and attending committee meetings. Mrs Pardiggle boasts:

> 'My young family are not frivolous; they expend the entire amount of their allowance in subscriptions, under my direction; and they have attended as many public meetings and listened to as many lectures, orations, and discussions, as generally fall to the lot of few grown people. Alfred (five)

who, as I mentioned, has of his own election joined the Infant Bonds of Joy, was one of the very few children who manifested consciousness on that occasion, after a fervid address of two hours from the chairman of the evening.'

Alfred glowered as if he never could, or would, forgive the injury of that night.

To involve your children in church life is an excellent aim. It has a lot going for it. You show them the importance of serving Christ. He is the centre – they are not. It teaches them to put others before themselves. It certainly does not hurt them to be bored occasionally: the world does not exist for their entertainment. And church life is a wonderful resource: there is so much to be learned there. Many church children see the church as their extended family, which is both brilliant and biblical. Many rich relationships, both with their peers and across the generations, can be made in the church family. Events such as holiday clubs or carol singing can be joyfully included in the children's programme. Such occasions and ensuing relationships may turn out to be crucial in influencing your children for Christ.

But Mrs Pardiggle's involvement of her children and enrolling them in the cause is actually a hijacking of their childhood. It is nothing short of exploitation. She is using her children to impress others and make a point. The unlucky Alfred, who remained conscious while sitting through a two-hour sermon, gained nothing from the experience but a sense of injury. Mrs Pardiggle is immensely proud of her children's ability to sit through boring adult occasions and 'give' all their pocket money away to good causes. But she is making two serious mistakes. First, she has ignored the children themselves and their needs. Secondly, she has focused entirely on outward behaviour and assumed that, because the children have been trained or frightened into sitting still and behaving impeccably, they are flourishing. But actually the opposite is true. What about Alfred's heart? What is going on there? Is he a cheerful giver? Does he love Jesus? Sadly, it would seem not.

For a minister's wife, the temptation to be impressive is immense. Because you have a high profile in the church and you know that people observe you, you have a heightened sensitivity to your children's appearance and their outward behaviour. Not only so, but you genuinely want to set a good example of family life. When your children look good you are relieved and gratified, maybe even proud; when they misbehave you are mortified and possibly furious. But remember Mrs Pardiggle and beware of the external focus. It can lead you to an unhelpful emphasis on dress or church attendance. It can delude you into thinking that, because your children can recite all the Holiday Bible Club memory verses, they are converted. It can lead to an appalling inconsistency whereby when they let you down in public you give full vent to your rage, but when they do the same thing in the privacy of your own home you barely notice. It can lead you to resort to bribery in order to produce the desired appearance, to hedge your children around in order to minimize the opportunities for misbehaviour, as a result of which they will not learn to use their independence well, for children need the freedom to fail because that is one of the ways in which they will learn and grow.

Most serious of all, Pardiggle-type behaviour can lead you to forget the heart, and that is the bit you have to be most interested in as a parent because it is the bit that God himself is most interested in (Isaiah 29:13). But when it becomes of paramount importance to you to prove yourself to be a good mother, then you are driven towards heavy control and manipulation. You find yourself making unhelpful comparisons and nit-picking and fault-finding. The result is an unmotivated and discouraged child.

Avoid the external focus. Attitude is everything.

Escapism

In order to avoid the foolish extremes of either Mrs Jellyby or Mrs Pardiggle, some ministers' wives totally immerse themselves in their children and behave as if the church did not exist at all except as a place to attend on a Sunday morning. Such a woman makes her children the focus of all her efforts and emotional energy. She always opts to stay at home with the children, and looking after them and meeting their needs is the sum total of her job description. Even when babysitters are offered as cover for a prayer meeting or evening service, she turns them down, so her husband regularly attends church events without her. She was extremely keen at the outset to make it clear that the church employs her husband and not herself, and she adamantly refuses to be forced into any minister's wife's mould: let no-one make any assumptions or have any expectations! Such a woman is secretly angry about the imposition of church on family life, sometimes even openly so.

My literary example here comes from Anthony Trollope's *Barchester Towers*. There we meet Mrs Quiverful, clergyman's wife and mother of fourteen. These children are not just her predominant interest; they are her *only* interest. When the Reverend Mr Q is passed over for a promotion her passion is roused, because of the children. Trollope describes the scene thus:

> We have heard of the terrible anger of the lioness when, surrounded by her cubs, she guards her prey. Few of us wish to disturb the mother of a litter of puppies when mouthing

a bone in the midst of her young family. Medea and her children are familiar to us, and so is the grief of Constance. Mrs Quiverful, when she first heard from her husband the news which he had to impart, felt within her bosom all the rage of the lioness, the rapacity of the hound, the fury of the tragic queen, and the deep despair of the bereaved mother.

Now in the context of the novel and the dreadful, political machinations of the ordering of the Barchester diocese, one has a great deal of sympathy for this minister's wife, especially with the responsibility of fourteen mouths to feed. Her rage is at one level absolutely forgivable. Have I not argued earlier in this chapter that a mother's responsibilities to her family are crucial and demanding? Mrs Quiverful is understandably passionate about her children, but she has no concern whatever for the kingdom of Christ. In fact she entirely ignores it; the church just exists to provide her family with a livelihood. Sinners that we are, we must be careful that immersion in family life is neither a convenient excuse nor a sinful idolatry. Followers of the Lord Jesus Christ are required to love Jesus more than they love their children (Matthew 10:37).

Perhaps we are afraid to get involved in church life through feelings of inferiority or because of painful past experiences, but the escape strategy is healthy neither for the children nor for the minister's wife herself. Motherhood does not mean child-centredness. To focus entirely on your children's needs, to order your life totally around their schedules, is very bad training indeed. Children are not the centre of the universe, nor indeed of your home (something we touched on earlier). So beware of giving them the impression that they have a right to your undivided attention from morning until night. While not wanting to fall into the errors of Mrs Jellyby, a certain amount of benign neglect is very good for children. It is how they learn to entertain themselves, to deal with boredom and the indifference of others, to get into scrapes and out of them, to think, to dream and to imagine. So never think that you have to lay on entertainments like a Butlin's Redcoat.

I recall periods of my life when things were difficult in the church. I confess that at those times I found it extremely therapeutic to wallow in the affection and fun of my children. But had I continued to immerse myself long term, I believe I could rightly have been accused of being merely self-indulgent. This was more about me than it was about them.

The escapist strategy is unhelpful for four reasons. First, we all have responsibilities beyond our own front doors, as neighbours, friends, church members and citizens. It is not fitting for any Christian totally to ignore these. Secondly, as members of Christ's body, the local church, we all have unique gifts. When we refuse to exercise them for the good of the church, the whole church suffers. Thirdly, we are in danger of making idols of our children and attempting to live our lives through them. This is an offence to Christ and a stumbling block to our children. Fourthly, we model to our children that church is optional, unimportant and an unnecessary inter-ference in our lives. But the church is in fact God's magnificent new creation; it is God's people, his household, and God dwells there by his Spirit (Ephesians 2:19–22).

I have set before you three negative ways of handling family responsibility as a minister's wife. But all of these pitfalls apply equally to the elderly-parent scenario. We have no business ignoring the needs of our parents because of church commit-ments. There may be a time in your life, as there was in mine, when you have to relinquish some church involvement in order to fulfil your filial duties. That too is Christian service. Although we will not be parading our well-behaved aged parent for the admiration of the church, we must be aware of the danger of pride in our good works. We must also be aware that a balanced approach to input with our parents is essential for our sanity and their good. That might mean that we do not do everything they ask us. Parents can be as manipulative and demanding as any child. They do have a right to your attention, but not exclusively.

It is possible to embrace and enjoy the most demanding seasons of our lives

As with so much in the Christian life, it is all a question of balance. Although not all elders and ministers are married, it is a qualification for eldership in Christ's church that any who are married must show a happy and orderly family life (1 Timothy 3:4–5; Titus 1:6). The way an elder will manage his home life well is, like the husband of Proverbs 31 woman, by delegating and entrusting to his wife most of what happens on the domestic front:

> She watches over the affairs of her household
>   and does not eat the bread of idleness.
> Her children arise and call her blessed;
>   her husband also, and he praises her.
> (Proverbs 31:27–28)

There is no single answer to the juggling question. When women ask me about being pulled in all directions and about being weighed down with so many demands on their time, they are hoping I will tell them to ignore the demands of A or concentrate on B. But I cannot do that. The best advice I can give you is to write your own job description before God, including all the roles you play. Suppose you write along the top of a piece of paper a list of all the assignments God has given you: child of God, wife, mother, daughter, friend, neighbour, church member, citizen. There will be more if you also have paid employment. Make those titles headings of columns, and in each write in order of priority the things you would want to do in any given week. Accept that you will rarely achieve all of them. Your aim will be to ensure that your effort is not poured exclusively into one column. In fact, refuse to proceed to the second item in any column until you have done the first thing in every column. Some of the columns will be shorter than others; some things on the list will be small in terms of time and effort, for example, a phone call or a few minutes spent in prayer. To demonstrate what I mean, on the page opposite is a rough and incomplete example from my own life currently. Our lives all have seasons so this schedule will need to be kept under review.

At present, because my children have grown up and left home, my input into their lives is small. My elderly mother-in-law, on the other hand, is high maintenance. This is God's particular assignment for me right now. I am not saying that you have to get out pencil and ruler and do this exercise – it is at best crude and imperfect, but it might help to make the impossible achievable.

Finally, let us attempt to learn some lessons from a godly woman from Scripture.

There are no ministers' wives in the Bible, and we need to be careful of drawing precepts from narrative accounts in Scripture. Nevertheless, it must be helpful to observe the attitudes and behaviour of one of the godliest women in Scripture: Mary, the mother of Jesus. She was highly favoured by God in being chosen to carry in her womb the incarnate Son of God and then raise him. But how did she respond to that unique and difficult assignment? She was after all a sinner

My job description before God

Child of God	Wife	Mother	Daughter	Friend	Neighbour	Church member	Citizen
Read my Bible every day	Pray for my husband	Pray for my children	Shop for mother-in-law and serve her main meal	Phone a friend	Pray and make time for a chat in the street	Attend the services and the prayer meeting	Read some of the newspaper every day
Pray	Feed him	Contact them	Sort out her money and bills	Meet someone for coffee and a chat	Help out at school	Prepare and teach Sunday school	Pray for the government
Memorize Scripture	Sex	Plan to meet up	Organize her transport to church		Visit my blind neighbour	Prepare for and attend the women's group	Write to my MP, as necessary

like us. There must be something we can learn about our lesser and more commonplace domestic struggles.

Learning from Mary

She accepted what God had ordained for her life (Luke 1:38)
'I am the Lord's servant . . . may it be to me as you have said,' was Mary's response to the angel Gabriel's message. What God expected of her was a huge privilege and an awesome responsibility. But she bowed to his sovereignty; she played her part. What we need to do as ministers' wives is embrace God's sovereignty in our lives. It is he who has assigned to us our demanding/delightful children, our awkward/amazing teenagers, our grumpy/grateful elderly parents. So much energy is wasted in resentment, envy and self-pity. But God has given you these tasks because he believes you can manage them. And in fulfilling these duties you are serving the God who made and redeemed you. Even when it is difficult, especially when it is difficult, bow to God's wise decrees.

She found comfort from a mature believing friend
(Luke 1:39–45)
Glad though she was to serve God in the way he had appointed, Mary's position was nonetheless vulnerable and lonely. The Bible does not tell us how the local community in Nazareth responded to her news, but the fact that Mary hurried off to visit her older cousin Elizabeth leads me to suspect that she found little sympathy among her Nazareth neighbours. You may have good friends and a good support group in the church – people who like you are handling the pressures of parenthood or daughtership – and, if so, strengthen those bonds and realize that you are not alone. Or if the pressures of the manse or rectory are adding that extra dimension of pain, then assuage

your loneliness by seeking out a good friend in another church, perhaps another minister's wife who will be a prayer partner for you. Elizabeth encouraged Mary, confirmed her calling, and gave her a sense of perspective on her assignment. That is what a good Christian friend can do for you.

She had a heightened awareness of the mercy of God (Luke 1:46–55)

God-centredness is what will keep us on the right track. All our best endeavours in family life will be fruitless without the centring on God which is evidenced by Mary's song. God is her Saviour; he is the mighty One, the holy One, the all-powerful One; and yet he has been mindful of her. Amazing thought! Sometimes we use our busyness and our rushing around as a way of justifying our existence, as though God were not a God of grace from whom alone any useful activity will spring. You do not have to justify your existence to God by rushing around and exhausting yourself in various ministries. Mary recalls that God is the one who performs mighty deeds, brings down rulers, fills the hungry. He doesn't need you in that sense. In fact, he can do very well without you. But it is our delight in him which will enable us, like Mary, to turn duty into choice and see our opportunities for service and even sacrifice as yet another evidence of God's mercy.

She was committed to her husband (Luke 2:1–7)

Joseph and Mary went together to Bethlehem. It is apparent from Mary's response to Gabriel's pronouncement that Mary was committed to God's plan for her life to be the mother of the Davidic Messiah as a married woman. Integral to that plan was her commitment to marry Joseph who was of the house and line of David. So they went together to be registered in

Bethlehem. They faced their assignment together. Our own marriages must be guarded and prioritized over every other family commitment. If caring for Dad is becoming too much, then this is a problem that must be faced together, even though in practice it may be you who is doing most of the work. In this way you are releasing your husband to serve God, so this is something you do for Jesus. And for this to be worth anything, you have to give cheerfully of your time and effort. Do not let the fact that at times the load you carry with regard to children or parents is unequally distributed cause you anxiety. Remain committed to your husband and the part he has to play in God's kingdom.

She was committed to the means of grace (Luke 2:22; 2:39; 2:41)

We see the mother of our Lord fulfilling the ceremonial law, going up to Jerusalem for the Passover, like any other humble believer. These things were established as priorities in her life's routines. So as ministers' wives, we too should prioritize the means of grace for ourselves. If Mary was not above these things with her unique and privileged role, then we are certainly not above the need to sit under God's Word, meet with his people and remember his death for us. We must observe these routines regularly and faithfully for their own sake, not mechanically or to be seen by others. We must take care to nurture our own faith in order to have the resources to share with others and in order to demonstrate to those whom we want to win for Christ the crucial nature of spiritual health.

She involved her family in a wider community (Luke 2:44)

Mary allowed her eldest boy, Jesus, some freedom. I love to picture this happy community outing to Jerusalem for the

Passover. Mary and Joseph did not hedge Jesus around or put him on a metaphorical lead. He was allowed to be part of that larger community. We as Christian mothers would do well to imitate this. If our elderly parents are willing, let them also be introduced to the church community. Allow others to help. Don't be too controlling. Both my children and my parents-in-law gained immeasurably from all kinds of associations within the church family.

She took her input seriously (Luke 2:50–52)
Even when Mary did not fully understand what was going on, as in the incident at the temple when her astonishing son had wowed all the top teachers, she still had work to do as a parent. Jesus was practically in his teens by then, but he still went down to Nazareth and was subject to his parents. So there was a continuing need for input by Mary and Joseph. Mary still oversaw his development in each of the four ways: intellectually, physically, spiritually and socially.

Balanced input should also be our aim. We are not to think that the intellectual is most important because ministers' children must excel at school and go to university; nor are we to be so heavy on the spiritual that our children think we don't have legs – we don't know how to kick a football. On the other hand, we must not neglect the spiritual for fear of the accusation that we are brainwashing our children. Social needs are important too. Are we so busy having people in the house for our own church agenda that our children never get a chance to invite whom they would like? It is good to keep those four areas in mind with elderly parents too. Sometimes I have been so occupied with meeting the physical needs that I have neglected the spiritual, intellectual and social. But reading with elderly people, praying, taking them visitors are no less important than the washing and dressing and feeding.

She had a reflective approach (Luke 2:19; Luke 2:51)

'Mary treasured up all these things and pondered them in her heart.' Let us not forget to savour the experience of raising our children and caring for our parents. It is so sad to have the attitude to life that says, 'I've just got to get through this or get this done, and then . . . ' These may be challenging times, but the days spent in caring for others are your life too, part of your story. Learn the lessons (even the painful ones) that God is teaching you and treasure the special moments. Sometimes we are so concerned with the desired end product or just our own relief and rest that we forget to treasure the moment. We are always looking for the fast-forward button. I was talking with a friend about the demands of caring for my mother-in-law, and I said, 'It is only going to get even more difficult as her frailties inevitably increase.' She agreed, but then she said, 'And then it will be hardest of all because she will be gone.'

Such wisdom enabled me to see that it was very foolish and pointless to wish the days away. Savour your relationships with your parents and children. Really enjoy the warmth and the fun. Even savour the sacrifices of love you make for them. That is a window which will close. One day there will be the empty bedroom and the vacant chair.

So let us embrace and treasure our temporary assignments. Thank God for them and use them to his glory.

For further reflection and action

1. What particular temptations (attached to life in the manse or rectory) are you facing? Of the three pitfalls, which is closest to home? How does the example of Mary help you to find a true perspective on your responsibilities?

2. List the various assignments/responsibilities God has given you at this point in your life. Taking these as headings, prioritize the various tasks relating to each one. Consider and pray over how you might achieve a good balance.
3. Thank God for the ever-changing diversity of your life. Pray now using Paul's prayer in 2 Thessalonians 1:11–12.

4. Privileges: Perks of the job

by Ann Benton

There was a period during my thirty years as a pastor's wife when I studiously avoided any ministers' wives' gatherings. The reason was that I had attended one which had left me with the sour taste of self-pity. All the way home my ears were ringing with the discordant echo of the collective moan. So I backed off, which was above all *my* loss.

I was overreacting. Such gatherings are an important release for the pressures peculiar to the pastoral life. They are the only place where you can safely say 'ouch' and be understood in the confidence of a sympathetic response. And that is all well and good. But we must beware of self-pity and not discount the immense privileges of being married to the minister. The job does indeed have its perks.

In writing them down I am also well aware that Christians are called to take up their cross. It was never going to be easy. Did you expect it to be? Recall Jesus' cryptic reply to the eager follower described in Luke 9:58: 'Foxes have holes and the birds of the air have nests, but the Son of Man has nowhere to lay his head.' Jesus does not want his followers to be under any illusion. If you want comfort, ease, security or popularity, choose someone else to live your life for. When you choose Jesus Christ as Lord and give him the right to direct your life, you are making a good choice, but not an easy one.

And yet there is joy. The greatest source of our joy is that our names are written in heaven. Jesus pointed this out to his excited disciples as they returned from a successful mission: 'Do not rejoice that the spirits submit to you, but rejoice that your names are written in heaven' (Luke 10:20). The most successful ministry on earth is not a greater source of happiness than the astonishing fact that the Son of God loved me and gave himself for me.

Yet there is joy in ministry. Sometimes we are ashamed to admit that we are actually enjoying ourselves. It is as if we believe that we have to suffer for our service, or that it is rendered worthless by our taking pleasure in it. Of course, we must beware of self-indulgence, self-satisfaction and all the other facets of pride. But we are allowed to enjoy serving the Lord we love. The fact that 'God loves a cheerful giver' (2 Corinthians 9:7) applies not just to monetary sacrifice.

Several items on my list of privileges may elicit from some readers a cynical 'yeah, right' or an anxious 'yes, but . . . '. I hope that such readers will accept that there will always be individual responses to some challenges and read on. There are also individual life-choices. For much of my life I have had both the luxury and stringency of being unwaged. The situation will be somewhat different if you are in full-time salaried employment. As I say, there are various life-choices, but still at least some of the benefits listed below will be perks any minister's wife will recognize if she has a mind to do so.

I am aware that with each perk I mention there will also be abuses and a whole heap of complicated and irritant factors.

Trust me, I am the last pastor's wife in the world to be dewy-eyed and sentimental. And this is an imperfect world. Dangers, trials and snares are part of the package. And yet, there is joy. Don't miss it. Don't let what you don't have rob you of what you do have. Here is what you have as a minister's wife:

A clear focus

If you love the Lord Jesus Christ your heart beats with a passion for God's kingdom. You want to see Christ's reign extended. Before you married a minister, or when he was a plumber or a barrister, perhaps you pursued your career, raised your family and in addition used some of your non-working hours for the church, attending, serving, even leading in some context or other. You loved to do it, but it was one among many other strands of your life. Now, by supporting your husband and being at his side, even if you make no other overt contribution to church programmes and still have a career, you have a very clear focus for your life. You are serving Christ's church. You wake up each morning and you know what you are about. This helps you to set your priorities and organize your day. It certainly lends clarity, reality and frequently urgency to your prayers. There is a race to be run so put on your running shoes and, as the athletes say, 'Keep focused'.

A defined role

I am not referring in the first place here to leading the women's meeting. I am talking about your care for your husband. Other people may not recognize this, but it is nonetheless true that if you did not do your job he could not do his. When he stands in the pulpit on a Sunday morning and begins to teach God's

Word, there is a sense in which you got him there. You are essential maintenance. And thus you are serving the kingdom. Without being on a single rota, you are 'doing something' in the church.

And as for those rotas without which no church could survive, you can pick and choose according to your skills and preferences. Yes, sometimes you will be plugging gaps, but how deliciously needed you will feel. How excellent to have something to do. Your inside knowledge will give you countless such opportunities for service. Your contribution will be welcome and significant. Other people, new to the church, may lack the confidence to put themselves forward and wait a long time to be invited to offer their expertise. But if flower arranging is your thing, then you have a platform and a whole block of floral foam with which to work. And as you roll up your sleeves to give help where it is needed, who knows what other gifts you will discover along the way?

A flexible lifestyle

You have to be there on Sundays, but on the other days of the week you and your husband have the ultimate in flexitime. To a large extent, you are free to organize your work to suit you. You may not have weekends off, but you will discover the delights of Monday afternoons when the children are at school. Your husband may be out on several evenings, but you will have him at breakfast and probably at lunchtime. He will be able to adjust his timetable to take one of the children to the dentist or cover for you when they are ill and you have to go to work. This is a massive perk, and you will learn how to use it so that arduous toil is interspersed with lighter moments. As one minister's wife advised, 'Work hard, play hard and never confuse the two.'

A partnership

If you want it and if it can be worked out logistically, then here is a great opportunity for working alongside your husband. There are some ministries which are well exercised jointly. Some couples do find it a strain to work together, but in my experience overall there is great value and a good deal of fun in it. Like Priscilla and Aquila, Paul's valued colleagues and friends, you are counted fellow-workers in your service for the church. Hospitality is an obvious joint activity, but visiting also is often easier and more appropriate as a double act. Experience has taught us that it is ill-advised and inappropriate for a minister to visit a younger woman alone. But you are not there simply to make up the numbers; you will make observations, supply conversation, recall details and offer sympathy to complement all that your husband says and does. Your intuitive insights will be helpful to his assessments.

All that is the observable aspect of partnership. No less valuable is partnership in prayer as you set aside regular times to struggle in intercession together for the church. Although your husband may have other elders to discuss plans, projects and people with, it is a significant and uniting exercise to spend time letting him bounce ideas off you, comparing observations and dreaming dreams together for the church.

Fame

Since you cannot be anonymous, find the upside of fame. It is not all bad. Just ask people who go through life unnoticed! You may not like the pastor's wife label, but it is nice to be recognized and missed when you are away. It may shock you to realize that people take notice of what you say and do. But use this humbly to be an example in godliness. As Paul wrote to shy Timothy: 'Don't let anyone look down on you because you are young, but set an example in speech, in life, in love, in faith and in purity' (1 Timothy 4:12).

A ringside seat

As a pastor's wife, you get a really good overview of what is going on. Most of us are naturally nosy, and other people's lives are fascinating. Of course I am not commending voyeurism: our knowledge is to be used to inspire thankfulness to God, inform our prayers and channel our practical expressions of love.

But who can deny the exquisite sense of privilege at being among the first to know about a birth, an impending marriage or even a death? Less dramatic events are also continually unfolding before your eyes: hospital appointments, first days at school, business trips, triumphs and disasters of every kind. These are all family events. They are your legitimate concern.

Most of all you will be observing spiritual progress. This was certainly a source of huge pleasure to the apostle John: 'It gave me great joy to have some brothers come and tell about your faithfulness to the truth and how you continue to walk in the truth. I have no greater joy than to hear that my children are walking in the truth' (3 John 3–4).

A door into people's lives

As well as a window you will have a door. To be able to minister to individuals at critical points in their lives is a rare privilege indeed. While others would like to help but hang back, your visit will not be thought strange but natural. You have been entrusted with these people's lives. Very often your presence is requested at a deathbed or another scene of crisis.

There is a sense in which perhaps you would rather not be there, yet to be asked to stand beside someone who is suffering is sobering and instructive and a time for massive dependence upon God. And you will be humbled when just turning up at a period of crisis is counted as a blessing. So I have been told, and the thought is astonishing to me.

Then there will be the good times, for we are instructed not just to weep with those who weep but to rejoice with those who rejoice. The weddings, the new babies, the recoveries, the anniversaries – in all of these you will play an undeserved part. It is hugely significant to prepare a couple for marriage or offer advice on raising children.

It is particularly memorable and joyous to be present at a new birth. Then you may be involved in the awesome task of nurturing and encouraging that young Christian towards maturity. As an older Christian in the church you have a scriptural injunction to train younger women, younger in faith or younger in years (Titus 2:3–5). That may mean Bible study in a one-to-one or group setting; it may equally mean practical help in the nitty-gritty of people's lives.

A family to love

They might seem a weird bunch when you first meet them. But take them to heart – they are 'those who through the righteousness of our God and Saviour Jesus Christ have received a faith as precious as ours' (2 Peter 1:1). And the funny thing is that as you live among them and get involved in their lives, as you thank God for them and pray for them, you will become inordinately fond of them. You will understand how Paul felt, for example about the Christians in Thessalonica – and he had been with them only a few weeks: 'How can we thank God enough for you in return for all the joy we have in the presence of our God because of you?' (1 Thessalonians 3:9).

A network of very fine people

Some will be before your very eyes in your own local church: godly people who live hidden lives of extraordinary courage and service. They do not make front-page news; they receive no medal. But you are privileged to have them around.

There are others who go off to difficult places and strike blows for God. Some of these you may on occasion receive into your home. Don't miss that opportunity either for yourself or your children. Pay attention and learn all you can.

I hope that you always bear in mind that yours is not the only church on the planet. If you keep abreast of the work of the gospel in your town, county, country and to some extent the world, you will know that you are not the only reapers in the field, even though the labourers may be few. All the more reason to stick together. There are conferences and meetings for ministers' wives, with or without their husbands. Take advantage of these and meet some extremely godly people, some of whom you might have the honour of calling friends. Such friends will stimulate and challenge you. Some will be admirable role models.

The prayers of the saints

Because you are in some sense high-profile, you will be prayed for, probably far more than other church members, and certainly far more than you deserve. On any given day in all sorts of situations, in bedrooms or on buses, your church members and other Christians will be mentioning you in their prayers. This is extremely humbling, very necessary and frankly wonderful. Never forget what you owe these people.

You will also know whom to approach when you need prayer support for a particular issue or crisis. Paul thanks the church of God in Corinth (a far-from-perfect outfit) for their prayers for him: 'On him [God] we have set our hope that he will continue to deliver us, as you help us by your prayers. Then many will give thanks on our behalf for the gracious favour granted us in answer to the prayers of many' (2 Corinthians 1:10b–11).

Worthy to suffer

If I have made Christian ministry sound like a night at the movies or a sun-drenched holiday, forgive me. If there is laughter, there is also weeping. In a world that did not want to know Jesus we can expect no better treatment. If it is not cool to be a minister of the gospel it is certainly not cool to be the minister's wife. Popular distaste for institutions in general, and for the evangelical church and its message in particular, will extend to you. In our culture such distaste will generally be covered by a veneer of politeness, but it will be there and you will know it. Probably the most you will suffer is the wrinkling of a nose and a turned back from time to time. Not much compared to the persecutions suffered by Christ's church worldwide. But that may change in the coming days.

And all rejection hurts, and we need to practise our response now with these trivial persecutions so that we are ready when the real ones start. The right response is a sense of privilege. What did the apostles do when they had been flogged for preaching the gospel? Complain of the injustice of it all? Change their message so as not to offend? Lie low for a while? None of these things:

The apostles left the Sanhedrin, rejoicing because they had
been counted worthy of suffering disgrace for the Name. Day
after day, in the temple courts and from house to house, they
never stopped teaching and proclaiming the good news that
Jesus is the Christ.

(Acts 5:41–42)

A slice of the action

You never really know what will happen next. You never know
whom God will bring along this Sunday for you to welcome
and get to know and speak the gospel to. You never know
whose heart the Holy Spirit will touch. Perhaps you will
become involved in someone's personal crisis: it is scary
because you really don't know what to say or how to help. But
it is also exciting to see what God will do in answer to your
prayers. This is after all an adventure of faith.

A phone call may change the course of your day or night.
It would be true to say this is inconvenient; it would be under-
standable to say it is annoying as your sleep is wrecked or your
plans are torpedoed. But it is also strangely invigorating.
When your husband became a minister, your life did not go
down the plughole; it became extraordinary – truly a life less
ordinary and never dull.

When Paul is in prison and thinks over life-and-death issues,
he chooses life because he knows that his life is significant. He
has the opportunity to make a difference: 'If I am to go on
living in the body, this will mean fruitful labour for me'
(Philippians 1:22a).

A life of fruitful labour beckons him in his work for Christ.
That is the life we are called to. Amidst the mundanity of the
coffee rota and the pew, the hassle of getting children ready
for church or the stress of rustling up bolognese for twenty,

don't forget to taste the sharp savour, even the exotic romance, of a life lived for God.

You never know what God will do.

For further reflection and action

1. Think through all the things you like about being a minister's wife, and thank God for each one.
2. How can you turn irregular work patterns to a positive for your marriage and family life?
3. Consider what you know about the joys and sorrows of your church members at the moment. Is there a practical way in which you could indicate your weeping with those who weep or rejoicing with those who rejoice? Pray for the opportunity to use, for the benefit of others, the fact that your input is considered a blessing.

5. Pressure points: For the sake of the kingdom

by Julia Jones

Born and brought up in Yorkshire in a non-Christian home, Julia had worn out her life's ambition to work with horses by the age of seventeen. Not able to think of anything else, she went off to train to teach. Through the work of the Christian Union she came to faith, and then became president of her CU, returning a few years later as a staff worker with UCCF. She felt a call to be a minister's wife, then fell in love with Daryl, who she soon discovered felt called to be a minister, but sensed he needed a wife first! Julia and Daryl believed God had called them both full-time into this ministry.

They are definitely downwardly mobile, humanly speaking, having served in ministry in a pretty village near Bristol, a suburb of Aylesbury and now inner-city Liverpool, though they would not be anywhere else.

Julia has authored of a couple of small books; she speaks at conferences, chairs the FIEC women's team and runs the course for student wives at London Theological Seminary. She is the mother of two student children. She enjoys swimming, trips to the theatre, and coffee with friends.

I have been known to say to my husband, 'Couldn't you get an ordinary job that you could leave at the office?'

But of course every job has its pressures. Long hours, shift work, deadlines, difficult customers, strained relationships – these are common complaints of many in secular employment. And those strains affect not just the employee but the employee's family too. So a discussion about the pressures of ministry life must start with the recognition that the minister and his family do not have a monopoly on pressure. When I was a new ministry wife I became friendly with a woman whose husband was a policeman. It helped me keep things in perspective: we both had lives that were affected by our husbands' working long, unsociable hours, but I did not have to suffer my friend's fear of her husband being caught up in violence. I did not have to ask that question she often asked herself: 'Will he come home tonight?'

This chapter will focus on the chief pressures of ministry life. They are not exclusive to pastoral ministry, but they may come as a shock to those new to ministry. Some of those pressures are self-induced; others just go with the territory. There is a sense in which we just have to get on with it and get over it. But that can be easier said than done, partly because by definition serving the church will render the demarcation line between home and church rather fuzzy. It is therefore much harder for a minister and his wife to leave their pressures outside the front door. Church life is personal, so things that affect the church will affect the minister and his wife personally.

Later in this book we will look more thoroughly at the emotional response to the most common pressures. (This is also covered in the final chapter on questions ministers' wives ask.) So this chapter will say less about the emotions involved. It will aim for the most part to deal with the pressures dispassionately. To the uninitiated it will say, 'These are the kind of things you can expect to handle', and to the experienced (or even jaded) it will say, 'You are not alone' and 'It is not just you.' In both cases there will, I hope, be some reason and encouragement to embrace your calling and some tips to help you keep going despite the occupational hazards.

Self-induced or self-aggravated pressures

The desire to please

This well-meaning instinct is overdeveloped in some of us and can land us in trouble. Especially when you are in a new pastoral situation you will want to win people. This makes you tend to say 'yes' to all kinds of requests, some of which are either unsuitable or impossible. Of course it is excellent to help out where we can, and there is certainly no place for being churlish. But a pastor's wife may find her presence and support requested far and wide. There may be the idea that the very presence of the pastor's wife lends an activity some kind of official status or higher profile. Absolute rubbish of course, but it is an undeniable fact that your attendance at this or that meeting will encourage. And indeed it is good to encourage. But set your own reasonable boundaries, even write your own job description according to your current responsibilities and gifts, and learn to say 'no' in the gentlest and most encouraging way you can to those requests which fall outside your present remit. We must not confuse serving people with pleasing people. In ministry, indeed in the Christian life, we have signed up to serving one another in love (Galatians 5:13). Serving people will mean that sometimes we do say 'yes' and put ourselves out for them, but not with a view to winning their gratitude or favour. Serving people might sometimes mean that we say 'no' to one request in order to focus on a previous commitment. It is never going to be possible to please all of the people all of the time. God has not called you to do that. You may be told a good deal about the former minister's wife and the various roles she fulfilled. 'All this is very interesting,' you must answer, 'but we are all different and I shall have to see where I can serve most usefully.'

The pressure to be perfect

Some ministry wives are keen to set an example; they realize that they are high-profile. They therefore feel that their homes, their cooking and their children should be perfect. The chapter on responsibilities to your family has explained why this is seriously bad news for your children. But it is also bad because of its impact on the church. Suppose someone achieved perfection in any of those areas. If their home or cooking were perfect, would you feel happy to invite them to your untidy home to experience your far-from-perfect food? Would you ask parenting advice of the parent whose children have never seemingly misbehaved, who are wonderfully well-balanced and who know no grades below A* and no sporting achievement below a gold medal? I think not. You would feel intimidated by such perfection and inclined to cover up, seeking support and advice instead from those whose lives were closer to your own. So perfection can be a barrier in ministry. People in our churches need to see homes that are welcoming, food that is gladly shared and children who are loved despite their faults. The best examples are set by those who face the realities of this broken world with faith, not with any pretence of faultlessness.

It is also bad news for you. Perfectionism is a well-trodden road to depression. There is a saying, employed by some who are aware that perfectionism is unhelpful and unhealthy: 'If a thing is worth doing, it is worth doing badly.' Or even: 'It matters, but it doesn't matter much.' Sometimes satisfactory is exactly what it says it is.

Church obsession

Simply because our hopes and prayers are so wrapped up in its progress, church can become an obsession of ministry wives. Ask yourself this question: 'What do I do that is not related to church?' As ministry wives it is easy completely to narrow our focus to church. It becomes our whole world. No wonder then that little ripples of discontent, minor oversights or failures threaten to engulf us. Those ministry wives who have some kind of external employment are less likely to encounter this pressure, but those who do not might do well to explore opportunities and outlets just to be members of the human race. Not only is this essential if we are to reach a lost world; it is crucial to our understanding of what it is like out there.

Christians sometimes quote: 'in the world, but not of it'. Sadly this can be an excuse not to engage with our community. Jesus did not want his people taken out of the world. He said, 'They are not of the world, even as I am not of it' (John 17:16). Perhaps that could be expressed as 'in the world and like Jesus in the world'. None can deny that Jesus was engaged with the world. He was found where the ordinary people were. He did not stand aloof with a condemnatory air, but got involved so that he could share the good news with compassion.

A young mother asked me what I thought she should do at the school gate. She explained that there was a group of women from church with whom she could stand, and there was also a group of very worldly women who were happy to chat to her. She was concerned that mixing with the latter group might give her a bad reputation. I asked her who she thought Jesus would choose to talk to. Who would he be most concerned about? And would he be concerned about what others said? She had answered her own question. Being with unbelievers gives us opportunities to be the salt and light we are called to be. It also keeps us in touch with how people are thinking; it keeps our gospel edge sharp.

But it won't always be plain sailing! A while ago, a group of mums from our toddler group asked me and a church mum to join them on a quiz team. As we often invite them to events at church we were pleased to accept – until the interval. Everyone was given a bingo card, not something that we were terribly used to. We glanced at each other, thinking we had better go along with it quietly. Then we were told it was 'stand-up' bingo, and we were even less familiar with that. Everyone had to stand up until a number on their card was called, and then they sat down. We both prayed that our numbers would soon come up, and thankfully they did.

It is great to listen to Christian music, read Christian books and go to Christian events, but it is also good to listen to secular music, read secular books and newspapers and go to secular events – whether they be sporting, theatrical or musical. Obviously we are to be wise in what we expose ourselves to, but in addition to being enjoyable and refreshing, these things will help us engage with others. We will be more rounded people who are more attractive conversationalists. We will be more in touch with the society in which God has placed us. And the pressure of thinking that the world starts and ends with our local church will be immensely relieved. So for the sake of your sanity as well as your witness, make room in your life for some kind of community activity. If you have schoolchildren, there are always openings on the PTA or board of governors. There are also allotments, book clubs, choirs, exercise classes, Neighbourhood Watch groups, Women's Institute meetings and so forth.

I decided to become a rep for a well-known cosmetics firm in a few local streets. It only takes a few hours a week, but it is a great way to get to know the locals. Avoiding the pressure to be church-obsessed will help us to serve the Lord and his church better.

The need to succeed

We take seriously the words of Jesus to his disciples in John 15:16. He has chosen us to go and bear fruit – fruit that will last. Whatever the size or state of the church to which we have been called, we are looking for growth: numerical growth by conversion and spiritual growth as members mature in Christ. Sometimes that growth can be painfully slow. Sometimes it can seem non-existent. Sometimes the Lord brings an excellent young couple to the church in answer to your prayers and they roll their sleeves up and are actively involved and then . . . they leave. Sometimes you might look round the church and say, 'Is this it? Is this all we get?'

That is when we start to beat ourselves up. Of course there may be some useful evaluating of the way things are done. But there is no formula for success in the ministry. The work of God is frequently hidden and rarely dramatic. No Christian leader wants to be in competition with other gospel-preaching churches, but many a minister of a small church is understandably disheartened by the numbers of local Christians who drive past the church's door every Sunday to join with a famously large and lively congregation in the next town. And if the man is disheartened, so too will his wife be. We know that God measures success differently, but we worry that he is actually passing us by altogether, just like those other Christians.

Sometimes there is an explanation and some action to be taken; often it is beyond our understanding. The only antidotes are the continual recognition that this is God's work, not yours, and the constant resorting to prayer. The pressure of the need to succeed is relieved only by a steadfast trust in the Lord and a commitment to continue to serve and honour him where he has placed you. What happens next is in his hands.

Circumstantial pressures

The end of weekending
There are some people who joke that ministers work only one day a week, and there are even some who really believe it. What is certain is that on that one day of the week the minister has to be in church and so do you. Which is fine, in general. Where else would you want to be? But if you were in some other kind of employment before the ministry, you might just start to remember weekends as they used to be: that Friday night 'schools-out' feeling when you throw off your work clothes and get ready to play. Other people in the congregation will go away for the weekend, and as a pastor's wife you will start to notice just how often that is. Meanwhile you remain at your post or in your pew. Attendance at services and prayer meetings, unless you have responsibilities that legitimately keep you away, ceases to be optional. This is what you signed up for. As I say, it is fine, but the realization that you have to be there can hit you quite hard.

Saturdays will also be affected, with at least some of the day taken up with preparation for services and possibly a certain gathering tension towards the end of the evening.

The unspecified hours

Most pastors have no idea what hours they work, and when they have finished of course they haven't. There is always a bit more tinkering with the message that could be done, another visit and certainly more praying. This can leave a wife wondering when if ever she has a right to a piece of her husband. 'He is doing the Lord's work,' she tells herself, and this, she unscripturally reasons, makes him kind of off-limits in terms of family demands.

On the other hand, if he happily takes an afternoon off to help her with the shopping or the children, sometimes it is she who feels vaguely worried that he is not doing enough work. What if they are spotted in Sainsbury's? Would a church member feel right to be aggrieved that this was not what the church paid the minister for, to be comparing the prices of frozen peas or choosing a joint of pork?

These things have to be worked through by the couple, preferably with the diary in front of them. It is essential that a pastor cares for his wife and family (1 Timothy 3:4), and this means giving them time. Most ministers take a day off in the week, and some are better than others at protecting it. It never works infallibly of course because people tend to have crises or even die without consulting the pastor's diary.

The smaller income

There is a vast variation between the salaries of ministers,[1] but most are paid less than their various qualifications would earn them in secular life. I remember when we went to our first church, we accepted the call before we found out what we were going to be paid – we thought we were being spiritual. However, having worked out the minimum we could survive on, with luxuries such as food, dental check-ups, haircuts, we discovered that the salary was a couple of thousand pounds short. The only way forward was to be honest and explain our predicament; the church met us halfway, but it was still a struggle.

It is important to be realistic about what you are willing to accept. While some churches are extremely generous, others are not. Many smaller churches are themselves seriously strapped for cash and struggle to pay a minister at all. It may be that God is calling you to make that kind of financial sacrifice. But you will need to have your eyes wide open and be honest with yourself, your husband and the church.

Sometimes we mothers regret the effect that lack of funds might have on our children. Certain makes of footwear or extra-curricular activities might be out of the question. Mothers are inclined to feel guilty that their husband's calling is damaging to their children. But don't overestimate that damage. It can be good for children to have less stuff. Their lives will be enriched in other ways. And God is good. Many pastors' wives testify to God's provision through surprising and delightful means.

I remember when our son's birthday was approaching, and he was in need of a larger bike which we could not afford. One day he came home from school saying that his friend was selling his bike and could he have it. We got in touch and arranged to collect it. When we arrived, the dad asked if we needed a girl's bike as well. We did. So he brought out a girly bike in pristine condition, which delighted our daughter no end.

But money will often remain a pressure. It may sound trite but it is true: this is an opportunity to trust God and prove him faithful.

The tied cottage
You may have been in the happy position of owning your own property before you entered ministerial life. If not, you might

be obliged to be dependent on whatever the church can do for you. Some churches can offer accommodation. And as many pastors would be unable to afford to buy their own home, the manse or vicarage can be a necessary asset.

But it can be difficult to live in church property. You will find that other members of the congregation are better acquainted with the house than you are; they will tell you about what the previous incumbents did and how they arranged their furniture. Such talk may make you feel that this is not your own home.

At a practical level, it is important to understand the ground rules of the arrangement before you move in. Who is responsible for what? Is there a budget for maintenance, and who sets this in motion? What if the boiler breaks down? Have you got to wait for the next deacons' meeting before anything can be done? How many meetings are expected to be held in your home or garden?

If you and your family are to make this house your home, not just a church annexe, you must not only understand the ground rules and set the boundaries, you must accentuate the positives to yourself and to your children. If it is a large detached house with an extensive garden, enjoy the experience of living in such a house, even though it is draughty, expensive to heat and you are hopeless at gardening. If you are within touching distance of the church building, enjoy the convenience. The best possible thing is to live in the community surrounding your church building. People will appreciate the fact that you are living among them, and there are wonderful evangelistic advantages to becoming part of the local community.

Make a mental decision to embrace whatever house you find yourself in. Do all you can to make it yours and put your own stamp upon it. Decorate it to your taste. Live in it as if you own it, even if you do not.

The claims of fame

As a ministry wife you will not enjoy anonymity; you will be categorized by the congregation as 'the wife'. In your neighbourhood, at your children's school or at the gym, once people find out, you will be 'the minister's wife' or 'the vicar's wife', with all the misconceptions and expectations these bring. You will not escape notice: not your clothes, nor your shopping habits, nor your children. People will be quick to judge your perceived inadequacies and weaknesses. Some of the attention will be benign, some not. Some people will avoid you in case you hit them with a big black Bible. It is best just to accept this. Laugh about it, enjoy it if you can and use it for the gospel. At least no-one will be surprised if you mention in a natural way what is going on at church.

If the limelight is something you deplore, beware of overreacting. Some pastors' wives are so determined not to be categorized that they deliberately flout expectations in an offensive way. There is no virtue in wearing old jeans and a sweater to a funeral just to make a point.

Interpersonal pressures

The husband

You are the only church member who goes to bed with the pastor. You are the only one who sees him at breakfast; you see him in grumpy mode as well as when he is at prayer. This is the man you love, but this is also a sinner. He is not as good a pastor as either he or you would like him to be.

Resist the temptation to tell him what to preach on or how to spend his day. Listening to his sermons, especially at first, can also be difficult. You are hypersensitized. Is that application too pointed, or not pointed enough? Didn't he tell that story only two weeks ago? It is well-nigh impossible to sit under God's Word and take it to heart as you should when you care so much about how the preacher is being received by the rest of the congregation. This calls for much self-discipline. Perhaps you need to start taking notes in order to focus on the message, not the man; perhaps you need to sit where you are not distracted by the sight of other people.

More seriously, there may be tensions between you and your husband when troubles afflict the church or when he becomes disheartened or down. These things too go with the territory. It would be nice to picture the pastor and his wife at such times finding in each other a mutual consolation. But this doesn't always happen. We need to recognize Satan's devices. Go to Job chapter 2. When Satan is permitted to afflict Job, he also in the same blow afflicts Job's marriage. Instead of sympathy and support, we find that Job's wife chooses accusation: 'His wife said to him, "Are you still holding on to your integrity? Curse God and die!"' (Job 2:9).

It is not easy to see your husband bruised and broken. And of course Job's wife has also bewilderingly suffered the death of all her children. She is angry. And sometimes when a pastor's wife sees her husband crushed, she is angry and looking for someone to blame. Job's wife's anger turns on Job, and beyond Job on God. Such a response may be mystifying to you. But some pastors' wives will recognize it. We need to see where this comes from: it comes from the pit.

The church members

When I was a teacher and we had a staff training day, we would often joke that school was a great place without the children. Sadly, sometimes we can also feel the same about church. Thankfully, it is not usually *all* the people. Most are delightful – winsome, supportive and hard-working. But there are some identifiable types in most churches:

- **The fault-finder/grumbler**

Some church members seem to delight in exercising the non-biblical ministry of criticism. Their first comment after a stirring message will be that the pastor chose the wrong tune to the closing hymn. Such members will enjoy airing their dissatisfaction at church meetings and make those occasions very uncomfortable for you. You will be amazed how worked up this kind of person can get about the thickness of the church mugs or the colour of the paint in the vestry.

- **The unreliable**

This is the one who enthusiastically volunteers support for a particular activity, but at the last minute phones up with a message about being 'too tired' and leaves you to carry on alone.

- **The monopolist**

This one homes in on you after every service and talks you into the ground. There are a dozen people you would like to catch up with, but it is really difficult to get away.

- **The demanding**

Some people drain us. They have so many problems, and if we have responded kindly once, they make it their business to involve us in every twist and turn of their complicated lives. The more help you give, the more they will want. They just love making their problems your problems.

- **The unlovely**

Every Christian church attracts its proportion of misfits and oddballs. That is because a church is one of the few places in the world where such people meet with kindness and accept-ance. But sometimes other church members get weary of trying to talk to people who are, to be honest, quite strange. So it falls to you, oftener than you would like, to make that extra effort.

The above are just a few of those you will encounter after every Sunday service. It can be, to say the least, a strain. People will tell us something about their uncle's neighbour's boss's son and expect us to remember all the details. Or it might be what course their child is doing at university or where they are going for their holiday. Sometimes I try to bluff and ask one or two leading questions, but sometimes I just admit I've forgotten and say, 'I'm sorry, you'll have to remind me . . .' Often people are happy to talk and tell you the details all over again.

How do we handle all of this week after week? The simple answer is that we must dress properly for church.

'Therefore, as God's chosen people, holy and dearly loved, clothe yourselves with compassion, kindness, humility, gentleness and patience' (Colossians 3:12). Compassion means that we will listen to the one whose life is a mess and enter their world. Kindness means that we will make a point of speaking to the unlovely. You were unlovely too, and Christ died for you. Humility means that we ask ourselves if there is any truth in the accusation the grumbler is making. And we will resist the urge to be defensive. And so on. You get the point.

When you choose to put on compassion as an act of will, you may find that your emotions catch up with you. But that does not mean that you must give everybody endless time, even if that were possible. Gently but firmly, set boundaries. Choose when you will give your time. Sunday morning after a service may not be a good slot to hear someone's woes. Arrange to meet on some other occasion. Don't agree to make such meetings regular. Stay in control. Meet a demanding person at a time when you know that you will have to leave in an hour, and make that clear from the very start. We can and should be firm. Usually the people who drain us are in need of boundaries. They may not like them, but they will respect us for them.

At a practical level some pastors' wives like to join their husbands at the end of a service at the door of the church. (This may not work so well if you have more than one door or if you have the kind of assemblies where people hang around slurping coffee and chatting for ages, in which case you may find it more useful to circulate.) But where it suits your situation it is a way of expressing that you and your husband are a team; it means you are there to offer women pastoral help; it means that people know where to find you; it ensures you do not get holed up with one person; it enables you to see people you might otherwise miss or who are avoiding you; it lends your intuitive skills to your husband's pastoral oversight.

Loneliness

The pastor's wife can be the loneliest woman in the church. Because you don't have weekends the opportunities to meet up with close friends or family who live elsewhere may be rare. Perhaps your husband's position sets you apart in the church and in the community, so that you are never quite one of the gang. Perhaps you are called to a church where there are no like-minded people or women at the same stage of life. Perhaps you have a church full of people who are glad to meet and greet you, but only when they want something from you – information, a route to the pastor's ear, help with their project or whatever. It can be disappointing, not to say wounding, to discover that, while you thought you were talking to a friend, in your 'friend's' eyes you were just a service-provider and she the client or customer. Any or all of those things, should you experience them, can contribute to a feeling of isolation and loneliness.

Some ministry wives will say that it is either impossible or inadvisable for a pastor's wife to have friends in the church. Such a mantra may be the bitter fruit of painful experience. I sympathize, but it still does not sound right to me. Jesus called his disciples 'friends' (John 15:15), and they let him down big-time. Who do we think we are? In any relationship worth having there is always a risk of being hurt. But we all need friends and are all called to be friends.

Nevertheless there are pitfalls and here are some ways to avoid them:

- In general, do not talk about the pressures of the job, as detailed in this chapter. It is neither helpful nor appropriate. And nobody likes a whinger.
- Don't be exclusive. If you have people you get on really well with, do not be always sitting with them and chatting to them at church events. There are other times for catching up with close friends.
- Be careful what you broadcast about your social life. You are entitled to a theatre trip with just a couple of friends, but you don't want to make others feel left out. Nor do you want to turn it into a church outing. Unless of course, you do!
- In conversation even with closest friends do not divulge anything that is not common knowledge to all church members.

Many ministry wives discover their closest friends outside the church. They find they can be more relaxed and open in such company. Look for or make opportunities to meet with other Christian women who are on the same spiritual wavelength as you. Perhaps via inter-church networks you can meet up with other ministry wives formally or informally, singly or en masse. These are great opportunities for honest sharing and the relieving of some of the pressure. We need others to make us laugh at ourselves, lest we take ourselves too seriously. And we need those who understand where we are coming from, whom we can trust absolutely and with whom we can pray. We are also encouraged by Scripture to exercise that ministry to others. You may find such a woman within your congregation but if not, look outside.

So these are the pressures. Like them or loathe them, we must learn to live with them. And pray for grace to do so cheerfully.

For further reflection or action

1. Do you ever fall into the trap of feeling that your life and your lot are harder than those of anyone else?
2. Which of the self-induced or self-aggravated pressures do you struggle with? How would you counsel you if you were someone else?
3. Of the circumstantial pressures, which cause you the greatest struggles? Bring these honestly before God, asking for his help in working them out for good in your life.
4. How do you cope with your husband being your pastor? How might you better enjoy and appreciate him in these different roles?
5. Think of the one person at church whom you find the most difficult. Commit to pray for him/her for a week and then go out of your way to encourage him/her.
6. Also this week make time to spend with a friend, whether by going for a coffee or having a long chat on the phone.

6. Her service for Christ: Using God-given gifts

by Jane McNabb

Jane was brought up in a Christian home, trusting in Christ for herself two days after her ninth birthday. She met Wes in Liverpool on the Christian Union stall at Freshers' Fair. It wasn't exactly love at first sight, but they soon became the best of friends and were married at the end of their studies. After primary teaching in Leicester for several years they spent an unforgettable year in Queensland, Australia. This led to a change in direction on their return to England. Wes became assistant minister in Chesterfield, during which time their daughter and son were born. Seven years later in 2002 they exchanged the delights of Derbyshire for London when they moved to The Slade Evangelical Church in Plumstead.

Although Jane has never returned to the classroom she still loves teaching, whether in her role of ESOL teacher at The Slade's English Corner, or through explaining the Bible to women by speaking or writing. She feels privileged to serve on the FIEC Women's Team, and committees for the London Women's Convention and the London Ministry Wives' Conference.

Jane loves trying new recipes while listening to music and then working off the results at the gym, in the pool or walking. When she isn't feeling quite so energetic she is usually to be found with her nose in a book or watching BBC period dramas with her teenage daughter.

In the early years of being a minister's wife one of my recurring prayers was, 'Lord, please make me a *good* minister's wife.'

'How admirable,' you might say, and I know that I desperately desired to be what I prayed for . . . but every time I prayed that prayer up would pop a picture in my head of a minister's wife I knew, one who seemed to fit the bill of being that perfect specimen.

Important as it is to have good role models, that image in my head was not particularly helpful. In fact that image was a lie. The woman existed, but of course her perfection did not. By the time I had finished comparing myself with her I found myself invariably in a state of despondency.

If the comparison game were an Olympic sport, many ministers' wives I know would be among the medal contenders. It is an easy game to play and practise, but the prizes on offer are far less desirable than medals: anxiety, guilt, envy, bitterness, exhaustion, loss of focus, a sense of overwhelming failure, puffed-up pride and many more.

I ask myself why I still find myself playing this game when it is so damaging. Here are some reasons:

a) It happens when I lose sight that I am saved by grace. I keep going back to the way I used to think before I was saved: that it is what I do that makes God love me rather than what Christ has already done for me. During those relapses into legalism I feel as though I am playing catch-up with all those impressive ministers' wives I know (and others who exist only in my imagination).

b) It happens when I become disgruntled with the body, the circumstances or the place God has put me in.

c) It happens when I neglect to discern, value and develop the unique spiritual gifts that God has given me. This third aspect is the focus of this chapter.

Unique spiritual gifts

The source of gifts

My guess is that most of us are familiar with those challenging and encouraging passages of Scripture that address the issue of spiritual gifts in the church (especially 1 Corinthians 12; Romans 12:1–8; Ephesians 4:1–13; 1 Peter 4:10–11). If we were to pick out the main points they would probably look something like this:

- The same God is Lord over all of us.
- The many and varied gifts are given at God's discretion and according to his grace to each of his children.
- Each gift is valuable and necessary to the growth, maturity and unity of the church.
- Each gift is given to serve a purpose and exists for the common good.
- Each gift is to be accepted with gratitude, obedience and enthusiasm.
- When practising our spiritual gifts we are to do so in God's strength.
- Gifts are to be used with reverence to the glory of God.

We are God's workmanship twice over! When God created me the first time, knitting me together in my mother's womb, he gave me certain gifts and abilities. Yet when he gave me a new birth in Christ, he gave me, and continues to give me, special *spiritual* gifts specifically equipping me for my new life in Christ. These gifts are for the blessing of the church and the extension of his kingdom, the greatest cause on earth.

God's people are not like a cut-out chain of two-dimensional paper dolls. Neither are we mass-produced clones, all designed to move like puppets as instructed. Rather, each of us is unique and special in terms of our gifting and calling. As Paul says, 'We are God's workmanship, created in Christ Jesus to do good works, which God prepared in advance for us to do' (Ephesians 2:10).

Many people might think that a woman married to a church minister would be in the perfect position to use and develop her gifts. Yet speaking from my own experience and through talking to other minister's wives, I now know this to be naïve. There are several reasons for this:

- A minister's wife still has her insecurities and inhibitions. If we were lacking in confidence before our husbands entered the ministry, those feelings are likely to intensify when we suddenly find (or imagine we find) ourselves under the spotlight. That can give us the desire to retreat. 'Better not to use and develop our gifts rather than fail' might be our policy or unspoken thought.
- We might be surrounded by women in the congregation who seem more capable, and we feel threatened by them.
- We can be so busy trying to fulfil that imaginary job description of the minister's wife in our heads that we rarely stop to assess what our individual gifts actually are. My prayer: 'Lord, make me a good minister's wife',

though well-meant, was too general. It would have been better if I had asked God to help me discern, use and practise the gifts he had given me to fulfil my role in the way he wanted me to.

- Maybe practising spiritual gifts was not something that was ever modelled to us.
- Our experience might be limited or the churches in which we have been involved may have restricted the use of gifts to certain areas and certain people. Perhaps we have seen specific gifts mismanaged, discouraged or overemphasized.
- We can feel trapped by the expectations of others to the extent that we are continually being backed into responsibilities that are unsuitable for us and sap us of our time and energy.
- We are so busy caring for family or working in paid employment (and perhaps both) that we are only just keeping our heads above the water with our responsibilities at church as it is. Developing our gifts seems to be a luxury that at the moment we just can't afford.
- We are in a church-planting or small-church situation where it really is all hands on deck with everything and anything.

Yet despite these hurdles, the Scriptures still encourage us not with the *idea* of gifting, but with the fact of it. Just because we ignore our gifts or fail to recognize them doesn't mean that God hasn't given them to us.

The discovery of gifts
So if that is the case, how do we define what our gifts are? Think about the following questions:

What is it that others consistently recognize in you?
What are you deeply burdened about?
What do you long to change or implement or do more of?
What inspires you to dream?
What do you enjoy?
What thrills you?
What gives you a buzz?

The chances are that in some way the answers show where your gifting lies. I am not suggesting here that gift-based ministry will always be enjoyable and pleasant, neither am I saying that we should be completely governed by our feelings, but generally we *are* to enjoy God's gifts. Surely that is what God wants. The problem is that, since Satan succeeded in tempting Eve to believe that God was mean and had withheld the best gifts, it is easy for us to believe that God doesn't want us to enjoy the gifts he gives us. Yet look at what James writes: 'Every good and perfect gift is from above, coming down from the Father of the heavenly lights, who does not change like shifting shadows' (James 1:17). And in 1 Timothy 6:17 we read that God 'richly provides us with everything for our enjoyment'.

One last question: What fits comfortably and suits you?

I am always puzzled by those items of clothing which say on the label: 'One size fits all'. How can that be? In reality some customers will be almost drowned in fabric, while others who are on the larger side will have their movements restricted! Hardly practical or flattering for anyone! Nor does it say much for the designer. What the label should say is: 'Fits all, flatters few'.

Thankfully our Designer's gifts are not like that. They fit comfortably. They don't overwhelm us, nor do they inhibit our movement. They are fit for purpose, look good and ultimately, it is the designer who gets the glory.

The use of gifts

Having established what our gifts are, we need to accept them gratefully from our wise and good God. We should take care not to be like the daughter of a woman I once knew. Despite all the hurtful things the daughter had done, that mother carefully bought, wrapped and sent Christmas presents both to her and her children. On Christmas morning one year she opened her front door to discover every gift returned and unopened, sitting on her step.

That story took my breath away, yet in reality have I always accepted God's gifts with joy? And having accepted them gratefully, have I always understood and used them as I should? Because whatever our gifting, there are some important things to remember.

- **They are gifts of grace** (Romans 12:6). They are given to enhance our service as we seek to work *out* our salvation. They are not given so we might revert to working *for* our salvation. This is tremendously liberating. As we cannot boast in our salvation, neither can we boast in the gifts that God has given us. In the Christian life we can never get away from this issue of grace. Spiritual gifts are no exception.
- **Gifts are not given to us so that we can lord (or lady!) it over others** (Romans 12:3), but to edify others. We will recognize that what we do is for the good of others.
- **Our gifts are given to us not to be worshipped, but to be used in worshipping our Creator** (Romans 12:1). Like anything else they can so easily become our idols. We need to be aware of that temptation and guard against it. We should never be so busy using and developing our gifts that we neglect our personal walk with Jesus. He is the reason for everything!

- **Using gifts never replaces obedience to God's commands.** Take Titus 2:3–5 for example:

> Likewise, teach the older women to be reverent in the way they live, not to be slanderers or addicted to much wine, but to teach what is good. Then they can train the younger women to love their husbands and children, to be self-controlled and pure, to be busy at home, to be kind, and to be subject to their husbands, so that no-one will malign the word of God.

We are all to be the older or younger woman described in this passage. We are not to use our gifts as an excuse to abandon our responsibilities at home.

As I write this my house resembles a rubbish tip, and dinner needs preparing. To be honest I would far rather continue writing than clean, but the truth is that I should put aside any gift of writing I might have for the next few hours, because my family and home need me.

If God has given us a command he will give us the resources to obey (even if we don't feel particularly gifted in that area). What is exciting is that often when we simply obey we discover gifts which we never knew we had. From there on, we discover that those gifts *enrich* the ways in which we are able to obey his commands.

Look at another command: 'Offer hospitality to one another without grumbling' (1 Peter 4:9). Perhaps you've heard of Elisa Beynon. As a young vicar's wife she offered hospitality even though she felt painfully underqualified. Fifteen years later she won a Waitrose competition to write a cookery book, and *The Vicar's Wife Cookbook* was the result. Writing in *Waitrose Food Illustrated* in August 2007 she said:

. . . I rashly married my very own vicar in 1993. Which wasn't at all clever: being someone who only ever wears extremely high heels, I knew, absolutely and completely, that I wasn't ready to don the lace-ups and take my place at the stove. More to the point, I couldn't cook and wasn't particularly into food. At university my only claim to culinary fame was the fact that I loved tomato ketchup on my broccoli. Or on anything, to be honest. Hardly an auspicious start to vicar's wifedom.

However, church and food seem to go together like PMT and chocolate. Get a bunch of churchies together and a big feed-up is always on the cards. So start to cook I did. And to my surprise and, in some ways, horror, so my love affair with food and the cooking of it began.

Elisa also says, 'Give me loads of people to cook for and I am happy. On my own, I'll eat from the fridge.'

I admit that this is a rather glamorous and slightly extreme illustration, and I must stress here that I don't believe that we necessarily have to cook well, or even at all, in order to offer hospitality, but I hope you get my point. To a lesser or greater degree this is the kind of surprising thing that happens to those who are obedient to Christ. How many of us find ourselves doing things that just a few years ago we wouldn't have dreamed possible, crushed and hampered as we so often were by our past failures, insecurities, laziness and fear?

If we are faithful stewards of the responsibilities God has given us, his way is to trust us with more opportunities to serve him faithfully.

In some ways this brings us back to what we noted earlier: that we can be so busy with family and work responsibilities that spending time developing our gifts seems a luxurious impossibility. Yet we need to look at the big picture here. These days will not last for ever. Thank God that in the long run nothing will be wasted, and it is sometimes during these pressured (and even frustrating) times that we are surprised to find resources and gifts that we never knew we had.

Being forced to step back from ministries we have been involved in for years offers us the space to reassess our gifting and the direction in which God is leading us. It is also at these times that others in the church often feel confident enough to fill the place we have vacated. It is their opportunity to discover and develop their own personal and unique gifts – often bringing freshness and insight to something that has become stale. And what if they don't? Well perhaps it is time to reflect on whether that ministry is still viable and appropriate.

These can also be good times to question whether our gifts and ministries have become our idols over the years or whether we have become self-important through what we do and what we're gifted in. Due to prolonged illness a very active and gifted friend of mine had to take an enforced 'time out'. She confessed, 'I have had to face how much of my sense of worth as a Christian has come through *doing* rather than through who I am in Christ.'

Gifts have their time and place

Moving to a new church is a great time to take stock and assess what we should do. We might be shocked to discover that there are plenty of gifted and godly women who are already *more* than adequately filling those areas in which we always imagined ourselves serving. Similarly, what we did in our previous church is not necessarily what will be required in the next one, and we need to take a little time as we settle in so that we make wise judgments.

Gifts are also often given for a season, and they will change, grow and adapt over the years. A few years ago I knew there was a need for a teacher in our Youth Bible Class. I had loved teaching that age group in the past, especially on youth camps, but in a matter of weeks I realized I had made a big mistake. I did not enjoy the lessons; I felt anxious, and then when my daughter made a very tactful comment one day about my approach, I knew I did not have the energy, the desire or the capacity to change. I pride myself in not being a quitter, and so it took a certain amount of swallowing that pride to admit finally that I was not cut out for it.

Around this time a new teaching opportunity arose for someone to teach the Bible to people learning English, and despite the challenges I absolutely love it. One of my helpers said to me one day, 'It is as if you come alive when you teach them the Bible, and so too do the students!'

Sometimes we need to learn that it is OK to fail, even as a minister's wife. In fact failure is often necessary to produce humility within us and drive us to a reliance on God in the areas we are gifted in. Failure is also needed at times to highlight the areas we are *not* gifted in and make us consider a change in direction.

My husband often says to new Christians on the subject of the church and discovering gifts, 'You don't know till you've had a go!' We have to be willing to try and maybe fail as we discover our gifting. By so doing, hopefully we will help to create a culture and safe environment for others in our churches to do the same!

Gifts help to regulate our priorities

Pagan worship was a flurry of sacrifices, rituals, giving and offerings because the people believed that such things would please their gods. Like all false worship it was relentless, exhausting, restrictive and lacking in joy.

Yet whether through pride or guilt, it is easy for ministers' wives to be swept along in a pagan-like frenzy of activity, doing everything and anything, often for the approval of others or to meet their own high expectations of themselves. Before they know it Jesus is not at the heart of what they are doing nor the reason why they are doing it.

I want to be sensitive here. Most ministers' wives I know are also busy because they have a desperate and genuine desire for Christ to be exalted and known. Yet whatever our motives, we should still have methods of prioritizing wisely so that we don't put extra and undue pressure on our personal walk with the Lord, our marriage, our family and our health. Careful consideration of our gifts, and when and how to use them, will help us in that process.

Some of us may think that if we step back and take stock then the Lord's work will suffer. There will be things in church that might stop or be hindered if we pull out. This is especially true in a small-church situation where we fear that the whole church might fold. But there are several potential problems with that approach.

- You are in danger of thinking that you are indispensable in the future of the church.
- You reveal a belief that God is bound to work only through particular ministries. (For example, I think sometimes we forget that there is not an eleventh commandment that states, 'Your church shall run a parent-and-toddler group'!)
- You may be masking obvious weaknesses in the church that might need addressing.
- You hinder reviews of whether particular ministries have in fact passed their sell-by date.
- You make it easier for others in the church to opt out of their responsibilities because you are covering all the bases.

When I started out as a minister's wife I felt that in order to be a good example to the other young women in the church I had to get stuck into everything, and they would follow my example. In reality that didn't happen. In fact they often felt intimidated. (I know that because on occasions they told me so – very politely of course.)

Imagine you are playing rounders with some other church members. There you are fielding at third base. As that first ball comes straight towards you, you move towards it only to be pushed to the ground by the fielder at second base who storms in to take the catch. This happens several times not just to you, but to the fielders on first and even fourth base. You start to lose confidence in your fielding abilities. 'If she feels she needs to cover my base,' you think, 'I can't be good enough for this game.' Not only does your confidence wane, but your concentration goes too. The fielder on first base loses interest and wanders off the field, and you start to wonder if you should too. Eventually Glory Girl is exhausted and fails to get to your base on time. You suddenly realize that it is up to you now, but due to a lack of confidence and lack of catching practice you completely bungle it. You feel stupid, and Glory Girl shakes her head in disbelief and disgust.

We know that a healthy church doesn't function like that rounders match. And we as ministers' wives should not behave like that fielder on second base, even if there is no-one on first base any more, and the person on third base doesn't match our expectations.

Here is another thought: just because I have a vision for God's work and perceive a need does not mean that I am the one to fill it . . . even though I might be fully capable of doing so. We need to remember that even Jesus turned down 'opportunities for service' because he prioritized other activities (Mark 1:35–39).

In the Old Testament, in 2 Samuel 7 and 1 Chronicles 17, we read that David had a brilliant idea. After God's presence in the form of the ark was returned to Jerusalem by David, he says, 'Look . . . I am living in a beautiful cedar palace, but the Ark of God is out there in a tent!' (2 Samuel 7:2 NLT).

Yet God points out to David that although a temple is in his sovereign plans, he has not actually asked him to do this. Furthermore, God tells David that it is not the right time and he is not the right person. This is a blessing God has reserved for David's son (one not even born yet), and it is all bound up with his promises and blessings for the future kingdom.

The lesson would seem to be that if you have a brilliant idea, a vision for God's kingdom, prioritize prayer over any other activity.

The levelling effect of gifts

Exercising our gifts helps to safeguard us from being defined by the title of minister's wife – either by ourselves or by others in the congregation. Church members can sometimes treat us with an inappropriate amount of reverence, and we can end up thinking of ourselves as some kind of Mother Superior. While I have no wish to detract from the valuable contribution we can make, it is salutary to remember that the minister's wife is never mentioned in Scripture and is not an office in the local church.

So when my husband retires or stops being the minister, although there will be some big adjustments and challenges to face, I won't be too devastated or feel that my main purpose in life has finished. My gifts do not cease with my husband's employment, even though the opportunities to exercise them might change.

At some point in church life most of us will come across the attitude that, 'This is what the minister's wife has always done and therefore it is what you should do too!' Every time we say, 'No. I am sorry but I will not be able to fill that gap you want me to fill because that is not my gift', we refute the misconception that we are different from any other member of the congregation.

To return to where this chapter started, rather than feeling threatened by the gifts of others in the congregation, or those of other ministers' wives, I can appreciate and thank God for them.

The eternal significance of gifts

In Luke 19:11–27 we read Jesus' parable of the talents. Although Jesus isn't necessarily alluding only to spiritual gifts here but probably to all the resources God gives us, the central message is clear. As Graham Beynon puts it, 'Life is shaped around a day to come. It is a day when we stand in front of Jesus and he asks us, "What have you done with what I gave you?"'[1]

In other words, our failures will be revealed, thankfully as 'forgiven failures' as Graham Beynon calls them, but revealed all the same. He explains, 'They will still be revealed because it is right that all of life is now seen with respect to Jesus.'[2]

This should not cause us to be paralysed with fear as the unfaithful servant seems to have been, but rather motivated by joyful anticipation of Christ's return. The servants who waited faithfully served with wisdom and delight. The result was that they were rewarded with more responsibility and honour when the Master returned.

Don't you long to serve your Master better, using the gifts he has given you? Don't you long to reach your full potential for him?

Well, have hope. Our Master is returning soon. Before we know it, we will be with him reigning in the New Jerusalem.

What else will we be doing? Revelation tells us that we will *still* be busy serving! In fact we will *always* be busy serving: 'No longer will there be any curse. The throne of God and of the Lamb will be in the city, and his servants will serve him (22:3).

I don't know how I will serve him. I suspect I will use some of those very same spiritual gifts he has given me here on earth. Yet without the curse of sin, time restraints and human frailty, I will be able to serve in the way I have always longed to serve on earth, but have never quite achieved.

For further reflection or action

1. Think through the questions under the section on discovering your gifts:

    • What are the gifts others consistently recognize in you?
    • What ministries and issues are you deeply burdened about?
    • What do you long to change or implement or do more of?
    • What inspires you to dream?
    • What do you enjoy? What thrills you? What gives you a buzz?

    Now list the ministries you are involved in. How do they match up?
2. How have you seen your gifting change and/or develop throughout your Christian life?
3. Meditate on and pray through 1 Peter 4:10–11.

7. Forgiveness and forbearance: Handling criticism

by Ruth Shaw

Ruth was born in Colombia, South America, where her parents were missionaries. She came to live in England when she was thirteen. Her ambition was to become a missionary somewhere in the Spanish-speaking world, so she did a degree in Spanish and Latin American Studies and then trained as a teacher. The door to overseas mission closed but she continued to be challenged about full-time Christian service.

While still a student she met her husband Spencer, also heading in the same direction, though at the time they were both *very* naïve about what pastoral ministry was going to entail! She worked as a primary school teacher for five years until their eldest son was born. A year later her husband joined the staff of a large church, and was subsequently called to pastor a church where he ministered for three and a half years. Since its foundation in 2005 Spencer has been pastor of Emmanuel Evangelical Church in Chippenham.

With four sons aged between nine and sixteen and an energetic border collie to keep them on their toes, life in the Shaw household is never dull! Ruth has a passion to see the women in her church grow and reach out to other women with the gospel. She organizes a monthly women's evening for them, helps to run a toddler group in her local community centre, and also does some supply teaching. She enjoys cooking, playing the guitar and getting stuck into a good book – occasionally escaping back into Narnia for sanity!

While I was recovering from a particularly difficult time in our ministry, I wrote to a friend describing the experiences we had just been through as some of the hardest years of our lives. I went on to talk about what it had been like at church, how people had behaved, and what people had said. My husband had come close to giving up ministry on a couple of occasions, and I had struggled hard outwardly to support him. I was, if I am honest, secretly hoping we would move to a different situation so that we would gain some relief. This was all happening against the backdrop of challenging personal circumstances. I have deliberately chosen not to go into detail about any of those experiences, partly because I have made the decision not to go back there, but also because the key lessons that I learned came from the way in which I responded to the events, rather than from the events themselves.

I had met a number of people in ministry who had faced similar challenging experiences, but who in time had come out the other side stronger and were characterized by grace and contentment. I too was eager not to find myself years on still trapped in a prison of regret and disappointment. The problem was, I *did* feel like a victim, I *was* angry, I *did* feel hurt and, though it took me a while to see it, I was bitter and resentful. I believed that God was in control. I recalled the story of Joseph in Genesis who, many difficult years after being sold into slavery by his brothers, had been enabled to see that what others had intended for harm, God had intended for good.

In some ways I could already see the evidence of that 'good' in the way our circumstances were working out, but I continued to struggle to make sense of what had gone before. I knew that the Bible told me to forgive, but it wasn't as easy as it sounded, and I wasn't actually sure how to. I shared with a friend that I was really struggling with the subject of forgiveness. She said that in a similar situation she and her husband had learned to pray that the Lord would bless those who had wronged them. I winced, but she said that although it was hard, in time I would. I came away thinking, 'I can't!' A bit like Jonah in his churlish response to God showing mercy to Ninevah, I had no trouble accepting that God was sovereign and had the right to bless whomever he chose to bless, and therefore I had no trouble with him responding to them in that way. But for me to do so just seemed so unfair! However, from that point, I began to think, pray and work through the issues and search the Bible for answers. It was in the latter that I found true comfort, practical advice and hope and began to learn genuinely how to forgive, forbear and better deal with criticism.

Learning how to forgive

Where do we start when the command to forgive touches very raw and painful wounds, and well-argued logic is the last thing that we are ready to listen to? Graciously, the Bible turns us not to a theory but to a person. So we go to a garden and see a man agonizing, 'Is there any other way?', yet still saying, 'Your will be done' (Matthew 26:36–42). Hours later we see him hanging on a cross, crying out: 'Forgive them' (Luke 23:34). As he dies he pays for *my* wrongdoing, he bears the disgrace for *my* sin against him, and his cry of forgiveness reaches me too!

I can see why David exclaimed,

> Blessed is he
> > whose transgressions are forgiven,
> > whose sins are covered.
> Blessed is the man
> > whose sin the LORD does not count against him.
> (Psalm 32:1–2)

We have deliberately rebelled against God and wronged him; we rightly deserve his punishment, yet he forgives us. He 'covers' our sins and we are told that he hurls them into the depths of the sea (Micah 7:19). He doesn't bring them up again or throw them back in our face the next time we fail, nor does he use them to humiliate us before other people or damage our reputation. He doesn't count against us what we have done either, but in an act of the will he chooses not to remember. He challenges our hearts too, not to harbour ill will or vengeful feelings towards those who have wronged us, but to surrender back our right to hurt others when they hurt us.

One of the hardest questions that I grappled with was whether or not we have to forgive someone who hasn't repented; after all God only forgives people when they repent. Clearly the relationship can only be restored fully if there is repentance. For true reconciliation to take place the wrongdoer must accept responsibility for what he or she has done and want to be reconciled. However, I came to the conclusion that the Bible did not give me room to wait for an apology before I dealt with my side of the issue. I was still told to love my enemies, bless those who curse me, not to keep a record of wrongs and, as far as it depended on me, to live at peace with everyone. It gently urged me to do so 'in view of God's mercy' (Romans 12:1). If while I was his enemy God's kindness led me to repentance, how then could I withhold forgiveness?

So how does all this work out in practice? We are all individuals who respond, even to very similar circumstances, in very different ways. The sins committed against us also vary both in their severity and their impact upon us. Clearly we are not the 'thought police', out to prosecute every wrongdoing we even suspect in others. What we are seeking to address here are those occasions where we feel we *can't* overlook things that people have said or done against us, because another's wrongdoing is playing so vividly on our minds. This in turn may be affecting our behaviour, our emotions and even our relationship with God.

What follows are some helpful principles on forgiveness that I am learning to work out in practice in my own life and ministry:

Principles of forgiveness

Taking time to work through the issues

Where a significant wrong has been committed, we need time to work through the issues. It hurts, and broken relationships do involve a sense of grief and loss that we need time to come to terms with. It is OK to take that time. There is the danger of a kind of spiritualized denial which bears more resemblance to pressing the escape button on a computer so that we don't have to think about the problem. It doesn't work – I have tried it!

The Bible helpfully presents us with authentic role models who take their doubts, their hurts, their questions and even their anger to God because they recognize that God is big enough to handle them. Their honest struggles give us permission to do the same. When I was struggling I could relate well to David's response when confronted by his enemies in Psalms 55 – 57. As he voices his concerns he doesn't mince his words, but he also reminds himself to cast his cares 'on the Lord'.

Recognizing where wrong has been done and calling it 'wrong'

Forgiveness is not saying it doesn't matter or pretending it wasn't wrong. It is appropriate to recognize where 'deliberate' wrong has been done and call it wrong. After all, the Bible calls sin 'sin'. One of the things I have found helpful is to write down what the issues are and what the Bible has to say about them. Then scrap the list because the Bible also tells me not to keep a record of wrongs.

Trusting God with justice and mercy

When we have been wronged we want justice, and that sense of justice is God-given. I really struggled at one point with a very strong sense of injustice, particularly having come to the conclusion that what had been done was wrong. Reading through 1 Peter one difficult evening I came across a verse about how Jesus had dealt with being unjustly treated by others: 'When they hurled their insults at him, he did not retaliate . . . Instead he entrusted himself to him who judges justly' (1 Peter 2:23). If those who have wronged us are Christians, we need to remember that Jesus has already paid for their sin and justified them. Either way the offence that has been committed is primarily against God, so we can place what he/she/they have done in God's hands and trust him with justice and mercy.

Repenting of anger, bitterness and resentment in my own heart
Very often other people's wrongs are the mirror in which my
heart sees its own reflection. As a sinner I know I tend to
respond sinfully to being sinned against. In my heart un-
resolved anger often replays the tape of others' wrongdoing
over and over again, and it begins to cultivate seeds of resentment that can grow into bitterness, which often bears fruit in
my thoughts and my actions as slander or even revenge. I just
can't keep that sense of outrage to myself, so I make others
pay with their reputation, or else I avoid them and give them
the silent treatment. Hebrews 12:15 challenges me to beware
of the roots of bitterness that can cause so much harm. The
dandelions in my garden helpfully remind me of my constant
need to seek God's mercy and forgiveness with this.

Praying for those who have wronged us
Genuinely praying for someone when we are still reeling from
the hurt that they have caused us is very hard and painful.
When we do pray, the temptation can be to pray 'our' agenda,
which is why the challenge to pray for blessing is so helpful.
Seeking good for those who have offended us, when what we
are naturally inclined to want is vindication, can feel really
harsh and unfair until we humbly see it in the light of the
cross. Only there can we begin to see 'our enemies' through
God's eyes of mercy rather than through the eyes of our pain.

Confronting where necessary the one we have been wronged by
We all know that when someone sins against us, where appropriate we are supposed to raise it with them privately (Matthew
18:15). There is a great danger that we may even be harbour-
ing a grudge against someone who doesn't know what they're
supposed to have done wrong. Either way it is a scary and
risky thing to do. It doesn't guarantee a gracious response

and may well open us up to further hurt and misunderstanding. However, if we want to see relationships restored we need to be prepared for difficult conversations.

Choosing not to remember and moving on

Forgiveness is an act of the will and not an emotion! This is hard because the debt doesn't just go away; we absorb it. However, there has to come a point of closure where we stop rerehearsing all the hurts and make a choice to move on. I know that where I have delayed making that choice it has been because I have given in to self-pity and other self-absorbed temptations, disguised but justified under the label of 'victim'.

Although we make the choice to forgive at a specific moment, it also needs to be reaffirmed and lived out daily because small triggers can so easily set the old tapes playing over and over again! In his book *Going the Distance* Peter Brain suggests three principles which I have found very helpful:

- 'I will not raise the matter again.'
- 'I will not tell others about it.'
- 'I will not dwell on the matter myself.'[1]

Corrie Ten Boom was given a helpful illustration when she was struggling to let go: to make the bell in a church tower ring you pull at a rope. The bell then takes a while to stop ringing. The challenge is not to keep tugging at the rope.[2]

Learning how to forbear

Most of our challenges are not in significant moments of wrongdoing but in the everyday niggles of church life. Take the individual who is constantly complaining or the teenager who stands by while an elderly woman struggles to move the tables and chairs. How about the man who makes his point through digs, underhand remarks and prayers with a hidden agenda, or the youth group worker who having discovered that it is hard work has decided to bow out rather than follow through on her commitment? Then there are those who have 'always done it this way' and the others who never want to do it 'that way'. Colossians urges us to clothe ourselves with compassion, kindness, humility, gentleness and patience, and then to bear with one another (Colossians 3:12–13). It implies that those various ways of showing mercy have to be worked at because we will all need bearing with in some way.

I wonder what picture you have in your mind of what 'bearing with' means? Who are the people and what are the situations in church life that tend to wind you up or discourage you? Who are the people about whom you feel embarrassed? I am increasingly learning to see that those uncomfortable moments and those challenging people have the potential to become some of my most valuable friends and allies in my journey to become more Christlike, on those occasions when I am willing to be taught by them. They have a way of exposing the sinful attitudes in my heart, so I have to turn back to the cross for mercy, forgiveness and strong help to love in a way that just doesn't come naturally.

Self-righteously praying for wisdom after one of 'those' kind of encounters, I read in James: 'The wisdom that comes from heaven is first of all pure; then peace-loving, considerate, submissive, full of mercy and good fruit, impartial and sincere. Peacemakers who sow in peace raise a harvest of righteousness' (James 3:17–18).

The reality is that in ministry we have signed up to the cost of loving front-line service to individuals who are self-centred, arrogant, stubborn, inconsistent, irritating – and remarkably like us! The encouragement is that because of the hope of the gospel, though we are sinners serving sinners, those same relationships can become increasingly ruled by grace.

Learning how to deal with criticism

One of the things that I particularly struggled with in the circumstances that I referred to earlier was criticism, especially criticism of my husband. If you can imagine criticism as bricks that people throw at you, you are faced with a choice of what to do with those bricks. You can throw them back; you can use them to build a wall to hide behind; or you can learn to catch them and trust God to use them to strengthen your character and build your faith. I chose the second option, withdrew, avoided the critics and kept people at a distance. Faced with a new set of circumstances I was deeply challenged that I could not love and serve people whom I held at arm's length. I also knew however that close contact with people would inevitably involve some future conflict, criticism and challenging relationships. I was conscious that if I did not learn to handle each of those better, I would only run, avoid people or hide as I had done before. I needed to learn to catch the bricks.

Criticism is not a simple struggle for any of us. On the one hand it is about what other people say, the reason why they say it and the way in which they choose to communicate it. On the other hand it is about how I respond to it: my feelings, attitudes, fears and expectations, and about wanting to honour God by reacting the right way but finding it hard to do so.

Here are a few simple principles that I am learning to apply to the way that I deal with criticism:

Accept that it is part of being married to a leader
An element of unfair criticism is an inevitable part of being married to a leader. Politicians, managers, teachers and

celebrities all face it to varying degrees, and Christian leaders are not immune. It has its roots in the Garden of Eden when human beings first questioned God's authority, so we shouldn't really be surprised when our husband's leadership is at times challenged. We are given a number of examples of leaders in the Bible who were criticized: Moses, David, Elijah, Nehemiah, and especially Jesus himself. We do need to learn at least to some extent to be resilient.

Develop simple strategies for responding to specific criticisms
Because criticism feels like a threat, the impulse to feel defensive and justify ourselves can be strong. Firing back may well exacerbate the problem rather than solve it. In difficult moments I have needed to find simple handles to slow me down and set a calm agenda for how I respond:

• **Stop and listen**
I have to take a deep breath and remind myself to keep my emotions in check. If I don't, I know I can so easily make assumptions and jump to conclusions without properly considering the issues that are being raised. James tells us we should be 'quick to listen, slow to speak and slow to become angry' (James 1:19). Proverbs also warns us not to answer before listening (Proverbs 18:13). I need to listen carefully to what is being said. Where necessary I need to ask for clarification and maybe even specific examples. If I summarize back to the critic what I have heard, it shows them that I have understood what they are saying and that I have acknowledged their concerns. I have found that time spent listening can diffuse a lot of tension, and that some people just want to be listened to! It may also be worth asking for time to think through a comment before responding.

- **Consider the source of the comment**

Who is saying it? Do I know why they are saying it? People criticize for a whole myriad of reasons and sometimes for more than one:

Constructive criticism is motivated by love and is an indication of true friendship: Proverbs 27:6 describes the wounds of a friend as 'faithful' (esv). Their input is considered and carefully given. It is designed to help us grow, by expressing concern and making us aware of where change might be needed. The giver risks misunderstanding, rejection and maybe an angry reaction. The willingness to take that risk shows that they genuinely care and that they take seriously the Bible's command to speak the truth in love.

Negative criticism may be designed to try to manipulate or control us, either by putting us down or by making us feel guilty, so that we alter what we do. It could be some people's way of punishing us because we are not giving them what they want or even because God is not giving them what they want. There are those who may do it to gain attention and others who simply have a negative outlook on life. It may also reveal deep personal struggles, so the criticism may be more of a cry for help than an attack on us personally.

We must however guard against guessing at people's motives or making false assumptions. We need to be especially careful of this in ministry because we are likely to be privy to a lot of very personal information confided in us. It is a trust, and we need to ensure we treat it as such, not just in what we don't say but in our thoughts and interpretations. When making an assessment about a person, we need to distinguish clearly between what we *know* factually about someone and what they *appear* to be like because of how they come across to us. This is a hard thing to do when we are on the defensive.

- **Respond with grace**

My willingness and ability to take constructive criticism is crucial to my spiritual growth and maturity. Proverbs 15:31 tells us that:

> He who listens to a life-giving rebuke
>   will be at home among the wise.

It also bluntly warns us that 'he who hates correction is stupid' (Proverbs 12:1). I do therefore have to consider if there is any truth in what is being said. If so, I must take responsibility and own up to my mistake.

There are often times when it is appropriate to disagree or to dismiss a criticism. The key question that I must then ask myself is how I can respond to this with honesty but also with grace. Even when the criticism is wrong or given for the wrong reasons, it is helpful to consider if there is something that I can learn from it.

- **Move on**

It is so important to remember that a criticism is an issue, but we are talking to a person. Moving the conversation on enables us to bring closure to the issue but keep the relationship open. I can think of several instances where after the conversation has moved on the individual has opened up about their real concern.

- **A few extra tips**

It is worth considering if there is some way in which we can involve the critic in the solution. Perhaps we could ask them what they would have done or what they suggest, give them the task of solving the problem or even ask them to pray for us. Some may then think twice before criticizing too hastily in future!

With emails it is worth applying the forty-eight-hour rule, that is, don't reply to difficult emails for forty-eight hours and *never* late at night. Emails are often not helpful when there are misunderstandings, and they don't smile, so when we have to use them we need to exercise extra care in replying to them.

When the criticism is about my husband I need to respect his integrity. However strong the inclination to defend him might be, this issue is his to answer, not mine, so I need to refer the critics to him. The church needs to know that I do not act as a go-between.

Responding appropriately to criticism is a steep learning curve for all of us, and we are bound to make a lot of mistakes. Our heavenly Father is gracious, so while we need to be teachable and learn from our mistakes we don't need to beat ourselves up over them.

Guard your hearts

As a sinner I am inclined to think the best about myself and the worst about others. Like Adam and Eve, trusting my own interpretation of the facts and then blaming other people comes naturally. I so easily form bad impressions of people who criticize me and then find it very hard to budge from those impressions. Ken Sande uses a very helpful illustration to explain how we tend to do that: where people have disappointed us or disagreed with us, we hold on to critical reports about them like Velcro and dismiss any favourable ones like Teflon. Where they have blessed us we tend to do the opposite.[3] The Bible firmly warns us to be careful how we judge others and urges us to take the plank out of our own eye *before* taking the speck out of our brother's eye (Matthew 7:5). In other words, we need to recognize that we too are sinners just as much in need of God's continual grace and mercy, struggling equally hard with other issues. When making judgments about people, I regularly have to check my motivation because I know it is mixed: am I using this information to support my theory, to justify my argument or to help me respond appropriately so that I build my brother or sister up?

Our heart struggle however goes deeper than our reactions. We serve on the front line of a battle! Our main enemy is *not* flesh and blood! The devil is out to derail or at least distract us and especially our husbands in whatever way he can. He will attack when and where he knows we are most vulnerable. One of the ways in which he does this is by deceiving us so we need to identify and fight the lies at the root of our struggle with criticism. Here are some that I have had to learn to fight:

- **That we have to prove ourselves to God**

Just like the other ministry wives who have contributed to this book, when my husband became a pastor somehow I felt we had to prove ourselves in that role. I suppose I felt we had to justify our existence and prove to God that we were up to the job, a bit like being on probation. Criticism implies that we have failed to measure up. How poor is my grasp of grace! How much I need to remember that the gospel has already judged us as failing miserably yet has justified us because of Jesus, not because of anything we could ever achieve. Not only that, but this defines our identity in Christ, not the role we fulfil. It tells us that we were chosen before the foundation of the world and are called to belong to Jesus Christ. It says that we have been lavished with the Father's love so that we really can be called his children, and describes us as royal priests with unlimited access to God's throne of grace. All of this is God's initiative rather than our effort so that he gets all the glory. We serve because of who we already are, not because of anything that we can add.

- **That there is no place for weakness and failure in ministry**

One of the problems with criticism is that it tends to use a worldly value system. It often compares us negatively with other people and judges us as being substandard. The thing is, we know our critics are often right: we *are* weak while others give the appearance of being strong and competent; we *do* fail where perhaps others seem to succeed; we *do* make plenty of mistakes where others appear to get it right, but the reality is that God uses weak people. Our weakness, resourced by his grace, often proves to be the best frame for his glory.

- **That we have to please other people**

Much has been said about this already in this book. But it is relevant here too. My husband has always said that you should do the right thing and let God worry about your reputation, but at times I do worry. I know that as a leader my husband is called to preach the Word 'in season and out of season' (2 Timothy 4:2). In other words his ministry must never be driven by popular opinion but by truth. In my heart though at times I want people to think well of us and approve of us too, and I fear the disapproval they might express in their criticism. Isn't there that part in all of us that is tempted to measure our value by the opinions of others? The Bible calls our inclination to please people for their approval the 'fear of man' and warns us that it *will be* a snare (Proverbs 29:25). Psalm 34 gives us a wonderful picture of where to turn when we feel afraid, and in Matthew 10:28–31 we are told that the answer is to fear God more than we fear other people. In practice this challenges us to see God as our key audience and his glory as our key goal. Of course that doesn't mean that we are oblivious to other people, but we serve others for their good because we love them, not because we need them to give us something in return.

- **That criticism is always bad for my husband**

Criticism can feel like a threat to our own or our husband's well-being. It is very hard watching someone you love being hurt by other people, especially other Christians. In those moments we need God's help and grace to believe that he is working on a bigger agenda than we can see. I regularly have to remind myself that my husband is the Lord's first. He has a right to do with him as he sees fit. I need to learn to trust his refining work in my husband's life and to accept that at times criticism will be the tool that God chooses to use for that purpose. I know that part of my struggle with this stems from the fact that it is very easy to hide behind a strong leader and even idolize them, until under attack you discover that they are more vulnerable than you thought they were. Those times have been such a helpful reminder to me that my dependence is supposed to be on the Lord rather than on my husband. *He* is meant to be my refuge, my strength and even my hiding place.

Dealing with unrelenting criticism

How do we handle those times when criticism has stopped being about individual concerns and feels more like 'jungle warfare', coming at us from every direction? What do we do when as a result of those pressures we find ourselves somewhere on the roller-coaster ride of faith, fear, anger, doubt, discouragement or even despair? At one point I felt so numb I even doubted that my faith was still real because it did not feel like it.

I found that the Bible did not trivialize that experience; in fact it offered me words to describe it which I would otherwise have been reluctant to use. It then showed me where to turn and urged me to hold on to what I already knew to be true of God and to continue to believe that he was good, despite how I felt. In his prayer in Psalm 77 Asaph asked the very questions I was almost afraid to ask. With hindsight he reminded himself that God had been with him, sustaining him, even when he had not been able to see his footprints next to him.

I recently found a copy of a letter that I had written not long after my difficult experiences to encourage a friend who was going through a tough time. I kept it because it summed up so well the genuine comfort that I found in the midst of my struggle:

When my broken world is in sharp focus it magnifies for me the preciousness of my relationship with God:

- When it hurts he is the God of all comfort who carried my sorrows.
- When others reject or turn their backs on me he is faithful and reminds me that I am not just accepted but chosen and loved unconditionally.
- When I am lonely he's an ever-present help.
- When I feel weak and my confidence is at rock-bottom his grace is sufficient.
- When I feel let down by those who are meant to support me the most he never forsakes me.
- When I have run out of strength and feel that I can't take any more he shows me real compassion.
- When I feel like I am just holding on he sustains me and puts his arms underneath to stop me falling.
- When I feel confused he assures me that he's working out his sovereign plan.

- When the road ahead is daunting he directs my steps.
- When I feel overwhelmed he reminds me that this life is temporary, his purposes are eternal and one day he will wipe every tear from my eyes.

I trust that you too will find comfort and encouragement in some of these truths.

How do we deal with criticism? How do we forgive and forbear? Increasingly we learn to see both ourselves and others in the light of the cross. The gospel changes the headlines that describe our relationships past, present and future from despair to hope: 'Guaranteed forgiveness for all past wrong-doing', 'That difficult relationship really can change', and the ultimate one: 'Welcome to *the* perfect church – presented to Christ free from all stain or wrinkle or any kind of blemish' (see Ephesians 5:27).

> So we fix our eyes not on what is seen, but on what is unseen. For what is seen is temporary, but what is unseen is eternal.
> (2 Corinthians 4:18)

For further reflection or action

1. In what area is God calling you to offer the same grace you have been offered in Christ?
2. What are the specific Bible truths you will need to learn to hold on to when you are confronted with criticism? How will you remember them?
3. How can the hope of heaven help to shape the way in which you continue to grapple with these things?

8. Encouragement: Modelling and showing encouragement and hospitality

by Julia Jones

Speaking at a women's day on the theme of encouragement I asked delegates to discuss in small groups how they had received this and how it had helped them. There was a great buzz as women happily shared their experiences. One group however seemed to have little to say and looked somewhat dejected. I went to chat with them and discovered that they were a group of leaders' wives. 'People seem to expect encouragement from us,' they said, 'but they don't think we need it too.' This served to illustrate the fact that however mature and experienced we may be or whatever role we have, we all need encouragement.

This chapter is about a ministry which all ministers' wives, whatever their gifts, can and should exercise, but I hope each one of us will receive encouragement from others too.

Why we need encouragement

Life in general can throw up many discouragements and sadly so too can church life. Discouragement is both powerful and destructive. I realized this negative power early on in our ministry. After a service my husband would receive many encouragements, but if there was one negative comment, even if it concerned something he wasn't responsible for, that would be the thought that would stick with him. We have often said that one discouragement needs at least three encouragements to balance it out. Sadly for many, it seems that the practice of discouragement and criticism comes far more naturally than that of encouragement. I suppose this is because negativity is what comes naturally to us as sinful human beings. We have probably all met those whom we could describe as born critics, yet far fewer are born encouragers. This all sounds pretty negative and disheartening, but the good news is that God is at work in us to make us what he would have us be.

We also have great examples to help us learn the way of encouragement, both in life and in the Bible. When thinking biblically, the character we would probably think of first is Barnabas. His real name was Joseph, but Barnabas was a nickname he had earned meaning 'son of encouragement' because he encouraged so much. Wouldn't we all love to be thought of as such encouragers that people started referring to us as Barnabases too! I love to read about Barnabas and see how God used him to build up his people. We first meet him in Acts 4 where we read that he was generous in giving what he could so that the work of God would be furthered (verses 36–37). In this instance he is giving his property. Being an encourager will at times mean being willing to give sacrificially what is ours to God's people or to his work. We also see how Barnabas was willing to give himself to others. In Acts 9:21–27 he was willing to accept Saul who had previously been a persecutor of the church. When others were wary of Saul, Barnabas took the time to get to know him, to hear how God had changed him and to recommend him to the church. This encouragement from Barnabas resulted in the changed Saul being greatly used to build up the believers.

We too need to be encouragers who are willing to take some risks, who are eager to recognize when God is at work in someone, and to encourage them and their gifts to be used in the life of the church. In Acts we see time and time again how Barnabas got involved in people's lives, rejoiced in what God was doing in them and encouraged them in their faith. One such example was in Antioch. Antioch had a very bad reputation, and it was said that any perversion could be indulged in there at a price. In Acts 11:23 Barnabas had been sent by the church in Jerusalem to check out the reports that God had been saving people in this immoral place. He does not arrive with a clipboard to make a written report; instead he takes time to get to know the people and to hear their testimony of God's work in their lives. Barnabas rejoices with them. How do we respond when we hear that someone has professed faith? Like Barnabas we also need to get involved and rejoice with them at what God has done. Many young Christians feel they don't measure up; for the first time in their lives they are aware of their sin and this makes them feel unworthy. To be like Barnabas we need to focus on where they have come from, the work of God already evident in them and encourage them to keep going, trusting God that he will complete the work he has begun.

This reminds me of a young woman I know who came from a background that was both neglectful and abusive. She looks at other Christians and feels a failure as she recognizes how much still needs changing in her. My role is to encourage her to see how far she has come and how great a work God is doing in her. She feels useless in many areas; it is therefore my role to take time out to help her recognize how God is at work in her and point out her positive qualities. To give her that precious commodity of time, take her out for coffee, show real interest in her as a person are ways of saying the positive that we all too often leave unsaid.

We also see the investment that Barnabas was willing to make in the lives of these young believers (Acts 11:25–26). I am sure he hadn't previously planned to spend a year in Antioch, nor had Saul whom Barnabas sent for to help him to disciple new converts. Saul and Barnabas were willing to have their plans and priorities turned upside down so that they might be useful to God. Again that is a challenge for us. How flexible are my plans? Am I willing to allow God to change them when he makes his priorities clear, when there is an opportunity for me to encourage someone to start walking or keep walking with Jesus? This is something both Barnabas and Paul were concerned to do. I love the verb in Acts 13:43: '*urged* them to continue in the grace of God'(italics mine). Being an encourager is being an urger.

All this leads us to attempt to define what encouragement is.

What encouragement is

Perhaps having seen how inspiring Barnabas is you too would like to be used like him. But what is encouragement? In the Old Testament the word that we use as 'encourage' comes from two Hebrew words which mean first 'to strengthen or to fortify' and secondly 'to strengthen the heart'. We see this in Joshua 1:6 where Joshua is encouraged to 'be strong and courageous'. In the New Testament the Greek words include the meanings 'to call to one's side, to beseech, exhort, comfort'.

So let's sum up what it means to encourage. Here is one definition: 'To encourage means to exhort and beseech one another to trust in God to comfort us and strengthen us courageously to live out what he has called us to.'

Or to put it more simply: 'Helping and enabling one another to live godly lives'.

Encouragement is concerned with both our practical and spiritual needs.

Encourage with practical help

I suppose it is pretty obvious. Encouragement might be as simple as being at a church event, seeing someone looking hassled and overwhelmed with the washing up and giving a hand. It might be cooking a meal for someone who is ill, moving house or has a new baby. Sometimes we can think this sort of encouragement is second-rate as it is not overtly spiritual, but I think God's example to us in the case of Elijah can help us to see that practical help is also a spiritual work.

Elijah had just had an amazing experience as he had trusted in God, and God had shown his power over the prophets of Baal. Whether Elijah's response is a low after a spiritual high or simple exhaustion, he is feeling so fed up in 1 Kings 19 that he asks God to take his life. God's response to Elijah is not to berate him and tell him he should trust more. Instead he allows Elijah time to sleep, provides a meal for him, then more sleep and another meal. God saw the whole person and recognized that Elijah's physical needs were important. Only after this time of rest and refreshment does God give him another amazing experience of himself before sending Elijah on his way to serve him again.

Sometimes as ministry wives we can be so concerned about people's spiritual well-being that we can miss their need of practical help and the encouragement that such help can give.

Encourage by example

The young Thessalonian believers are described as models to other believers (1 Thessalonians 1:7). That may have surprised them; it would certainly have pleased them. Whether we like it or not, our lives will be seen as examples to others in our churches. Our responsibility is not to live with an eye on what people may think, concerned always that we are giving a good impression. If those are our aims, then people will only see us, our strengths and our weaknesses. Instead, what the Thessalonians were praised for was for living transparently godly lives: lives that were not perfect but seen to be in the process of transformation; lives that were inspired by a living relationship with Jesus. Work wasn't done in an effort to be well thought of but as an outworking of their faith. This is the example we too need to set. It is a challenging goal but it has a simple solution. We need to ensure that we are walking day by day in relationship with Jesus, being fed by his Word and with our love for him growing as we continually recognize all that he has done for us. We need to be willing to be open about our walk with God. People will see how our faith is worked out in the good times and perhaps more challengingly in the tough times. We read in 1 Thessalonians 2:8 of the apostle's delight in sharing his life with others. For us, this will mean taking the time and making the effort to develop relationships, to look for opportunities to share with people in practical tasks and in spiritual communication. Small groups or one-to-ones can be a great way to develop such relationships.

I am involved in a women's Bible study group. It is a great privilege to meet regularly with a group of women aged from mid-twenties to ninety. As we study, we apply God's Word to our daily lives and struggles; we laugh and cry together as we open up about our cares and concerns, whether these be the frustrations of a young mum or the anxieties of a grandmother. Having met together for a few years now, the trust between us has grown and there is a lovely intimacy as we have shared one another's challenges and joys. In these situations it is not just that we encourage others as they see our example of faith lived out, but we too receive encouragement as we have the opportunity to see God at work in others.

Encourage with God's Word

This leads quite naturally to thinking how we might encourage with God's Word. As I have already said, we need that daily feeding on God's Word as well as what we receive in church if we are to be effective encouragers of others. Through preaching, teaching in other situations and private study we will receive blessing, help and comfort. It is great when we can find ways to pass this on to others. So often when talking with someone about their need, the Spirit will remind me of something I have learned that I can pass on as a help and encouragement to them. Sometimes it might be appropriate to write out a verse and put it in a card, an email or a text for someone who we feel it would be of help to. At the end of a service, as opportunities present themselves, speak about how you have been challenged or encouraged. Do not keep quiet about God's blessings. Share them and thereby multiply them. Whether it is preaching in church or teaching in some other setting, encourage the teacher by briefly saying how the teaching has helped you, not to flatter, but to encourage them so they can see God at work. Yes, you can even do this with your husband when he has preached.

Encourage with prayer

It is good to let people know that you are praying for them, not to make you look good but in a way that expresses your love and concern. When someone has asked you to pray about a situation, ask them how things are going and assure them you are still praying. When someone shares a concern, offer to pray straight away if that is possible even if it is over the phone. When someone prays for or with us, we are encouraged to trust God more. The definition of encouragement which I proposed earlier suggests helping people 'to trust in God to comfort us and strengthen us'. This is what we are about. When you know someone is facing a tough or challenging situation, they will be greatly encouraged by a phone call, a card, an email or a text assuring them of your prayers.

Encourage with rebuke

Perhaps rebuke does not seem to fit with the different aspects of encouraging that we have considered so far, but it does do so if we go back to our earlier definition of 'helping and enabling one another to live godly lives'.

There's a well-known part of the Bayeux tapestry where the bishop is 'encouraging his troops' by poking them with a spear. There are times when encouragement needs to be tough, and this is where rebuke comes in. In helping one another to live godly lives, there will be occasions when a rebuke is both necessary and appropriate. In such situations we always need to guard ourselves against being those natural critics I spoke of earlier. Rebuke must never be with the desire to prove ourselves right. It must be done with prayerful consideration, in the context of an already-established relationship and with the desire that the recipient will be helped to walk more closely with God. Any rebuke must be made from scriptural principles, as 2 Timothy 3:16 indicates. It is not my opinion that matters, but God's perspective that needs to be appealed to. It should also be done with affirmation of what is good and right; our aim is not to destroy people, rather to help them regain that closeness with God and his people and be useful examples to others.

I think of one young Christian who seemed to have lost her earlier enthusiasm. She attended meetings only rarely. After praying about this I went to see her and gently raised my concerns. I was extremely nervous about doing so. However, she actually thanked me for raising this, admitted that her private Bible reading had also slipped and asked for some advice to help her get back on track.

Encouragement opportunities

Encouragement and visiting

As ministry wives we may take on a certain amount of visiting. When doing so, whether it is someone who is ill, housebound, feeling down or seems to be drifting, it is good to be clear about our aims. Visiting is not about making us feel better because we have been good and have visited – though we are often encouraged by those we go to encourage. I have recently been visiting a woman who lost her husband very suddenly and unexpectedly. We have talked a lot and we have wept and prayed together. I hope I have encouraged her but I know she has certainly encouraged me as I have seen her faith and deep trust in God in spite of her difficult circumstances and how low she is feeling at times. When someone is going through trying times, talk about trusting in God's sovereignty even though it may feel like holding on by the fingertips. We know God has a strong grip on us. In the case of some elderly people it is a real privilege to hear of decades of walking with God and how he has worked in their lives. Our aim should always be to encourage the one we visit to keep on trusting in God. Some will be struggling with this in the face of circumstances. Others will be trusting, but perhaps because of loneliness they just need fellowship; they will find contact with another believer and the opportunity to talk about the Lord and pray together such a great help.

When visiting someone resist the temptation to let them know that you have suffered more than they have, even if you think this is the case. And always avoid gossip. Also, do not expect someone who is ill or has chronic pain to discuss strategy for some group they are usually involved with at church – they would struggle with this when experiencing such suffering. Our visit should be an expression of God's care.

- **Time**

It is good to plan how long we feel is appropriate. When someone is very ill or in pain, a short visit will be appreciated much more than a prolonged one: ten to fifteen minutes is often appropriate in such situations. Your aim should be that your visit does them good rather than wears them out. If you are visiting someone who is unable to leave the house then a longer visit is usually gratefully received. Sometimes such a visit can be hard to end as your company is appreciated, perhaps as their only human contact that day or even for many days. It can be good to let them know towards the end of the visit that you'll be going in ten minutes as leave-taking can be hard. For those in such situations, physical contact, a hug, the touch of a hand can speak volumes.

- **Practical help**

I love it when visitors bring flowers: they are a visible reminder of their care. But sometimes other practical helps can be more useful. If the person who is ill is the main cook, or a carer is being stretched by extra responsibilities, or there is a new baby in the family, a simple meal will be greatly appreciated. It is good to take something that could be eaten immediately, stored in the fridge for the next day or frozen, in case a number of others have done the same as you. People will often say, 'Let me know if I can do anything.' There is rarely a response to such general invitations. Instead it would be good to ring before your visit and ask if you can pick up some shopping. When you are visiting you could ask if you could take any washing or ironing or even do some cleaning. I am not suggesting that you become a regular shopper or cleaner, but at times of crisis this practical help can really encourage. For those who are spending long hours in recovery, a DVD, a light novel or a biography might be a useful distraction. But don't ask if they enjoyed it as they'll tell you if they did and hopefully won't if they didn't! For those who are housebound it can be good to take something such as the church magazine or notice sheet so you can talk about what is going on or give them a sense of connectedness with the fellowship. This may lead into praying together about fellowship needs.

• **God's Word and prayer**
I will often talk about something I have been reading in my devotional time or about something from a recent sermon. Remember you are not there to give a sermon but you can chat through a passage. Sometimes it can be good to have written out a verse that you think might be of help so that you can leave it with them. Be willing to share how God is working in you, challenging you, helping you, and pass on your blessings. With elderly people whose minds and memories are not as sharp as they once were, the words of an old, loved hymn can bring comfort. I remember one woman who was really struggling with depression, yet as we sang

together the words of an old hymn, accompanied by the
sound of her oxygen supply, her face lit up as the familiar
words ministered hope to her.

Sometimes it can be good for both of you to pray, but if
someone is ill or in pain, you will need to do the praying. Keep
prayer brief, as pain and illness can make concentration very
hard. Ask what the person would like you to pray for and don't
forget to ask again on a subsequent visit. Include praise of
God: your aim is to help lift their eyes from their situation and
concerns to the God who cares and can help.

As we visit we need to keep in mind or aim to encourage
those we visit to rest and trust in God. We should also be
concerned that they will hope we return rather than hope we
never do!

Encouragement and bereavement

I recently visited a woman in the last days of her life. When I
arrived she was in bed in a living room which was crowded
with family members. I read from John 14 about the Father's
house that has been prepared for us. She beckoned me closer
and whispered, 'That gave me more comfort than all of these
[family members].' What a privilege it was to share such a
precious moment with her and see her trust in her Saviour as
she knowingly faced death. Having said that, dealing with
death and bereavement is never easy, especially if it is the death
of a child, a young person or an active adult. It is natural to
be concerned as to how we will handle it: what can I say? what
if I cry? These are natural fears but we must not allow them
to keep us away from the bereaved. However hard we find it,
to keep away will make things harder for them. Of course
sensitivity is needed as we all respond differently. Some need
quiet and space, and this should be respected: keep a visit to
minutes. But also be ready to pick up signals when things

change and the bereaved person needs company. Most will appreciate any efforts you make to show concern, even if you don't feel you got it right. Some bereaved people have said that they feel like lepers as people avoid eye contact and conversation, and this hurts. Sometimes they just need you to sit with them, hold a hand and share their tears. A friend described this as 'the ministry of presence', often much more important than words. Be careful not to use trite sayings like: 'It's all for the best'; 'He's had a good innings'; or 'God has his reasons.' These don't help when the loss is a gaping wound. Be careful not to talk about your own loss either. You might have lost a parent or a partner too, but no two relationships are ever the same. Most bereaved people, either earlier or later, will want to talk about their loved one. Mentioning the name in appropriate situations will be a comfort because they don't want their loved one to be forgotten. It can be good to verbalize what they are feeling in acknowledging that the depth of the pain is a result of the depth of relationship that they had.

Sadly some Christians have misinterpreted 1 Thessalonians 4:13 when it says, 'We do not want you to . . . grieve like the rest of men, who have no hope.' Grief is a natural, normal and necessary process, even for Christians who have lost Christian loved ones. Of course there is the comfort of the certainty of heaven, but the pain of separation is still very real. Christians will rightly grieve for other Christians but without the hopelessness of those with no promise of heaven. Our role is to be there supporting and loving through such tough times.

We need to recognize that there is no set time for people to 'get over' a death. If the person who died was close, they will probably never fully do so. But people do eventually learn to live with loss and take up normal life again, even if this means that some will always 'walk with a limp'. Here I am thinking particularly of those who have lost a parent while still teenagers or have lost a young child or a partner many years before they expected to.

The practical helps that we considered in the previous section are all relevant to the bereaved person. Practical help can be a lifeline: it can be hard for people to cope with mundane chores at such times. Be wary of ending support too soon. Often everyone rallies round for the first couple of weeks, but many would really appreciate such support for a little while longer. However uncomfortable you might feel around the bereaved, do something. The bereaved feel isolation, loneliness and despair; don't compound this by choosing to leave them alone as well. A very practical thing you can do is note the date of the death and send a card the following year to let the bereaved person know that he or she is still in your thoughts and prayers.

Encouragement and hospitality

I am passionate about hospitality because it has been such a great encouragement to me personally throughout my Christian life. Converted as a student, I first experienced a Christian home through hospitality. Far more important than the food, which I am sure did me good at the time, were the love, fellowship, example and acceptance that I received.

• Keep it simple

The problem with hospitality is that we can see it as a performance. We get concerned about the state of our house, the quality of our cooking or the behaviour of our children. Yet hospitality should be about opening our homes to one another, being willing to share our food and our time. This liberates us from feeling the need to put on a showy meal. I am sure that when Jesus accepted invitations to eat in people's homes he wasn't concerned about how tidy they were or if the food was perfect. His concern was to spend time with people to encourage them in their understanding of and love for God. So stick to what you would normally cook for the family and keep it simple so that your time is spent with people rather than pots and pans.

- **Choose a time and style that fits**

Hospitality is something that is required of leaders (1 Timothy 3:2). As a ministry couple this needs putting into practice, yet there can be great flexibility in how you do it. Some find Sunday lunch after the service a good time to invite people back, yet some ministers find that if they are preaching twice that day it can be too much – especially as they get a bit older! Over the years we have used different opportunities at different times. If it is a Sunday dinner we find that it works best for my husband to be in the kitchen finishing things off while I do the chatting; he finds he needs a bit of space to unwind after preaching and he makes great gravy! When our children were young they loved the variety of people who would come to eat with us. It was great for them to get involved in hospitality, perhaps setting the table or preparing food – all good training for the future. Once they became teenagers they were less keen on having so many visitors, so we adjusted how we did things. They are still expected to eat with us and usually still enjoy this; they are still expected to help with the meal and they do this very willingly; yet they are free to go off to their rooms afterwards though at times they will choose to stay and chat some more. Weeknight meals can be good for parents of young children as they may appreciate leaving them with a babysitter and having uninterrupted time to talk. Don't let the food stop you: a take-away or a pre-prepared supermarket meal are fine for hospitality.

- **Be a servant**

I have already said that hospitality is not about showing off our home or our cooking skills, rather a servant ministry that creates opportunities to encourage. Often at church we see people for relatively short chats but in our homes we have time to get to know one another better. Sometimes people can feel wary of visiting the minister's home. But usually when they experience relaxed, homely hospitality they will become more at ease. A good question to ask of those you don't know well is how they came to know the Lord. This helps move the conversation on to more spiritual matters. Another useful question is how they came to the church. This can be an opportunity to talk about how they are fitting in and whether they are finding opportunities to grow and serve. You don't always need prepared questions. Sometimes your guests will take the opportunity to ask you questions on a variety of topics. It is also good to have time to talk about and understand people's daily lives, their families and their work. And people are often encouraged to know that you are interested in and concerned for them. Sharing our homes is another aspect of 'sharing our lives' (see 1 Thessalonians 2:8).

- **The open home**

What about the question of whether or not to have an open home where people are constantly dropping in? Some people have such a ministry, and it can be well used especially with young people. There needs to be caution, however, as it would be inappropriate for your husband to welcome a young woman into the home if you weren't there, and vice versa. There also needs to be consideration of how such a set-up will affect family life: I remember a young woman saying how she felt her parents had time for everyone except her. For a minister working from home endless interruptions can make sermon preparation difficult. We don't have people constantly in our home though we do have plenty of invited guests. We all need to work this out for ourselves, with prayer and godly wisdom.

- **Widen your guest list**

Be careful that giving hospitality does not create cliques, so make your invitations as wide and varied as possible. We have often found that those we were a little nervous of inviting as we thought it might be hard going have brought great blessing as we have heard of God's work in their lives.

A great thing about hospitality is that it can be contagious. If the hospitality you give is simple and relaxed this can encourage others to give it a go, and so this ministry of encouragement grows.

- **Bear the cost cheerfully**

1 Peter 4:9 shows great realism when it says, 'Offer hospitality to one another without grumbling.' There will be cost as we welcome people into our homes. There will be some cost in monetary terms, yet we can view this positively as part of our offering to God. There will also be the cost of effort in extra shopping, cooking and washing up. Sometimes there is the cost of people making a mess, whether by dirty footprints on a new carpet or a leaked nappy on the settee. But the great thing is that as we seek to encourage others by offering hospitality we often gain so much more ourselves. Indeed, as we give hospitality we may be welcoming angels into our homes (Hebrews 13:2). Angels are messengers of God; perhaps God will speak to you through those whom you invite.

The greatest encouragement to me is that Jesus became one of us and shared our humanity, then paid the price to set us free to know and to serve him. We need to live our lives following in his footsteps, 'sharing our lives', living for him and for one another.

For further reflection or action

1. Think of someone in your fellowship to whom you could 'say the often unsaid' to encourage them in their role or ministry.
2. Are you willing for God to change your plans so that you can be an encourager of someone? Can you think of an occasion when this might happen?
3. Whom are you particularly encouraging in their walk with the Lord?
4. Is there someone with whom you could share how God has been speaking to you? Send a card, an email or a text to do just that.
5. Plan some spiritual encouragement for someone you intend to visit in the near future.
6. Plan to offer hospitality, however simple, to someone who could do with the encouragement of receiving your time and care.
7. Think of someone who has encouraged you and thank God for them.

9. Humility and contentment: The minister's wife's view of herself

by Lizzy Smallwood

Lizzy was never convinced that she would *ever* get married, but if she did she used to claim she wanted to marry a sound and sexy vicar. In her youth and enthusiasm it just seemed the perfect way to do full-time Christian ministry in an unpaid capacity . . . in partnership with the man of your dreams . . . hmm.

Having trained as a teacher and completed her probationary year as a secondary school art teacher, she jumped ship and began ministry as a Christian youth worker, moving from churches in Romford to Stockton-on-Tees to Peckham and then back to Romford. It was while she was on the Cornhill Bible Training Course in 1991 that she met Simon and . . . he seemed to fit the bill! They have been married since 1994.

They began their ministry together in Burton-on-Trent. Then while hoping for a job in a church in the North-East they accepted a job in a church in Dagenham, Essex. They have been there since 1996. They now have three children: Sam, Ailie and Beatrice. Lizzy spreads her time thinly between being a mum, a vicar's wife (i.e. doing full-time Christian ministry in an unpaid capacity, in partnership with the man of her dreams), a part-time foundation stage teacher and teaching women the Bible. Her favourite way to relax is with a good book and a cup of tea. Her favourite night out would be the cinema, closely followed by any karaoke opportunities . . . and she just loves making soup.

Have you watched any award ceremonies recently such as the Oscars or the BAFTAs? It has become fashionable in acceptance speeches to say, 'I feel really humbled to be standing up here tonight . . . '

And you the viewer think, 'Yeah, right! What they really mean is: I feel really proud to have just won this prestigious award.' But they can't say that, can they? So they say the complete opposite: 'I feel really humble . . . '

Ministry wives find themselves, if not literally, metaphorically on a platform. This can affect their view of themselves.

Psalm 131 examines the whole question of pride and humility as the writer takes a look at himself. This is one of the shortest psalms to read but one of the longest to learn – it takes a lifetime of repentance to live it out every day.

My heart is not proud, O Lord,
  My eyes are not haughty;
I do not concern myself with great matters
  or things too wonderful for me.
But I have stilled and quietened my soul;
   like a weaned child with its mother,
   like a weaned child is my soul within me.

O Israel, put your hope in the LORD
  both now and for evermore.
(Psalm 131)

Well, my first reaction when I stumbled upon this psalm was, 'Isn't it proud to say I'm humble?' It is just like those people at the Oscars: 'I feel so humbled to be here today . . .'

You have got to be pretty sure of your standing before the Lord and your own heart to be able to say, 'My heart is not proud.' This is a psalm attributed to David. It may be that he wrote it at a time before he was king of Israel when Saul and his courtiers – maybe even David's own brothers – were accusing him of being an upstart, an arrogant nobody, a shepherd boy. How dare he claim to be God's anointed one?

Whatever his reason for writing – and it is a beautiful psalm – I don't think that David is being proud by saying, 'My heart is not proud . . .' I think this is the end product of much soul searching. It is about a journey. It shows the progress of the child of God from pride and 'spoilt-bratishness' to humility and contentedness, a child totally trusting in his heavenly Father for everything.

We get it so back to front, don't we? We are so naturally proud and worldly – we are going to take some convincing that humility and contentment are the highest attainment for the Christian minister's wife. They are the attributes that grow from a true understanding of God's grace. Pride on the other hand is the arch enemy of grace and kills it dead. Pride has no need of grace.

The psalmist says his heart is not proud

What has struck me again and again as I thought about this is how much our pride is at the root of nearly everything we do that is wrong. In the Garden of Eden when Satan said to the woman, 'You will not surely die' (Genesis 3:4), the truthfulness of God was called into question by his enemy, and ever since that time when we sin we are basically calling God a liar. And that is because we are proud. We have an inflated view of our own importance and we think we know best.

So let us spend a bit of time thinking about pride, particularly the type of pride we will be prone to in Christian ministry. We may be proud in our opinion of ourselves, in our positions of Christian leadership. Here are some questions to discover whether you, as a minister's wife, might occasionally have too high a view of yourself. Ask yourself:

- Do you hate to be criticized by people in your congregation? Are you over-sensitive, quick to take things the wrong way?
- Do you hate others pointing out your faults . . . or your husband's? Are you always on the defensive?
- Do you loathe it when you believe you are not being treated as you deserve to be? This even has an official title now: It's called an 'entitlement attitude'. We don't just see it in ourselves in church either. How about when we are driving: we are furious if someone cuts us up on the road. How very dare they? Don't they know who we are?
- Do you fish for compliments, wanting to know how well you are doing?
- Do you boast about your achievements, although of course you are very subtle in the way you do it? (You would perhaps find a way to drop into the conversation something about this visit you made or that family you are supporting.)
- Do you ever tell lies, especially little white lies, or exaggerate to make yourself look better before others?

And it is not just loud extrovert ministers' wives (like me) who are proud. Shy people can be just as guilty: I wonder if you can relate to any of the following ministry situations:

- When you meet a new group of people are you anxious about whether or not you will fit in ?
- Have you ever had a conversation with someone where you said something that later struck you as stupid or thoughtless? You keep playing the conversation over and over in your mind, convinced that the other person must think less of you because of what you said. The more you think about it the more embarrassed you feel.
- Are you afraid of making mistakes that will make you look bad in other people's eyes? We are all proud in different ways. And this usually springs from a fear of people that is greater than our fear of God. Whole books have been written on this, and it has already come up not a few times in this book, but here's just one example: the way we compare ourselves to other ministers' wives.
- Do you ever look at others and wish that you were more like them?
- Or do you ever look at others and feel good about yourself because you're not like them? Is your heart proud about what God has made you, where he has placed you in ministry?

Pride can work both ways:

Either you may feel a bit chuffed with yourself for landing a gorgeous *vicary* husband and a 'nice' church and a *huge* vicarage in Whomping in the Willows . . . 'because you're worth it'. Or maybe you're miffed because you've ended up with a duff husband in a horribly difficult church in a pokey manse in Grimsville – and you think you deserve better.

Yet if we just stop for a moment and reflect on who we actually are in God's eyes and the reality of our position before a holy God, our pride should burst like a bubble.

'Who am I really?' Someone who actually was destined for hell before Jesus rescued me. So who am I to think any church placement, any house, any town is below me?

It is truly unfitting for the sister of Christ – who made himself nothing – to want to be admired and given a position that carries honour. If it is bestowed on you – hooray! That's great. But let's not be ambitious for ourselves – or our husbands. 'Remember that many through wishing to be great have failed to be good.'[1]

Then notice in verse 1 that the psalmist also claims:

His eyes are not haughty

Here is another challenge to our pride. You see, pride has its home in our hearts but it shows itself in our eyes. Jesus said they are the window of our soul: we cannot veil the pride in our eyes (see Matthew 6:22–23). So how might this show itself in our Christian ministry?

We may look with contempt on those at our church who we think are beneath us, socially or intellectually. You may have people at your church who are a million miles from you culturally. It is so easy to treat these folk as inferior in the way you relate to them, by your speech, your expressions or your body language.

Where we work the level of dysfunction in some families is breathtaking. Some people round here make Ozzy Osborne and the Simpsons look like fine, upstanding members of society. And I confess that sometimes in church on a Sunday morning or at the school gate I listen to people talk about their lives, and my proud heart has one of two reactions:

either I want to walk away – tell them to stop, shhhhhh – 'I don't want to hear any more about your messy life, thanks.' Or I'm tempted to patronize them to try and impose some nice neat *Lizzy* solution on to their chaotic existence. It takes an act of will and a work of the Spirit to listen with humility, not to look at them with contempt, with haughty eyes, but to love them – because Jesus bothers to love me . . . and them!

And then in many of our churches there are the well-off, successful, nice people. Then the danger is that our haughty eyes look up with envy at them. We may think, 'I should be enjoying that lifestyle, the lifestyle I deserve . . . What on earth am I doing as a minister's wife?' Our eyes can be full of resentment and jealousy: we cannot share in people's delight in life because we feel hard done by – we are just plain green. This may be especially true if we or our husbands did a high-powered job before going into the ministry, and we have had to downsize radically.

Then, of course, there's the whole 'status' thing. We want people to treat us with the respect we think we deserve, to honour us, for who we are or who our husband is. The truth is some people will think you are 'special', to be looked up to and adored. They want to put you on a pedestal. And the problem is – you want to stay there.

We want to perpetuate the myth that we are in some way more important than other mere mortals. Even though we know that we are supposed to be serving the Lord and his people, we find ourselves self-serving again. Our proud hearts love a bit of hero worship.

There are some people who love clergymen. They just love the office of Minister of the Church of England – it's a sort of men-in-uniform thing except it is men in dresses.

You may have found that where you work some people, particularly women, sort of idolize your husband almost to the point of obsession. They want his undivided attention at the end of every service; they sulk if they don't get it and slag him off to outsiders in a sort of 'I-know-the-minister-intimately-but-he-doesn't-care-for-me' sort of way.

When they phone to talk to him and get you, the disappointment in their voice is heartbreaking: 'Oh it's you. Oh I suppose you'll do . . .'

There is one woman in our church who loves the fact that my husband is posh. Now thankfully it is quite comical. But the danger for Simon is the temptation to play up to it, to let people believe in his other-worldness, because it is nice when someone thinks you are Dagenham's answer to the Pope.

You or your husband may be faced with similar situations in your ministry, where people look up to you in an unhelpful sort of way that flatters your pride and confirms your sneaking suspicion that you are indeed wonderful! *Beware*, for it will show in your eyes.

Then the psalmist declares, 'I don't concern myself with great matters or things too wonderful for me.'

He has learned not to meddle

He seems to have learned the secret of accepting that God our Father is in fact superior to us, and that his hidden purposes and sovereignty are not actually our concern!

This may come as a bit of a surprise to those of us wives with a large streak of control freak: that actually God doesn't need us to tell him his business and perhaps make a few well-meaning suggestions as to what he might do.

This writer has learned the true meaning of 'Your will be done'. If only we could be a bit more like Mary the mother of Jesus and say, 'May it be to me as you have said', rather than 'May it be to me as I rather cleverly suggested.'

Robert Murray M'Cheyne put it beautifully: 'It has always been my aim and it is my prayer to have no plan as regards myself; well assured as I am that the place where the Saviour sees meet [fit] to place me must ever be the best place for me.'[2]

So let us allow God to gaze into our hearts and fill us with real humility. Let's be amazed again that he's willing to use people like us – like *us*! – and let us get our grubby paws on anything to do with his kingdom, his Word, his people.

It is truly awesome that he lets us work for and with him. And of course it is only because of what Jesus has achieved for each one of us

- clothing us in his righteousness
- giving us his Spirit who works in us
- giving us gifts

that any of us can do anything of use.

So let us give up our pride, our haughtiness, our meddling and let's ask the Holy Spirit daily to produce in us the fruit of humility. This springs from a right view of ourselves and a correct understanding of God's grace through our Lord Jesus.

We must examine ourselves and see how pride and haughtiness run through our actions and our attitudes like the blood in our veins, and then we must confess it as the sin that it is. We must admit how serious it is and stop treating it so lightly. In other words, we must fear God.

The best way to do this is to go to the cross.

The Welsh preacher Dr Martyn Lloyd-Jones helpfully put it like this:

There is only one thing I know of that crushes me to the ground and humiliates me to the dust, and that is to look at the Son of God, and especially contemplate the cross.

> When I survey the wondrous cross
> On which the Prince of Glory died,
> My richest gain I count but loss
> And pour contempt on all my pride.

Nothing else can do it. When I see that I am a sinner . . . that nothing but the Son of God on the cross can save me, I'm humbled to the dust . . . Nothing but the cross can give us this spirit of humility.[3]

Contentment and humility go hand in hand

This humility has a partner. Verse 2 describes it:

> But I have stilled and quietened my soul;
>> like a weaned child with its mother,
>> like a weaned child is my soul within me.

The psalmist says he has become as subdued and content as a child *whose weaning is fully accomplished.*

Now I was rubbish at breastfeeding so I didn't really have to experience this weaning thing. In biblical times children were weaned at about the age of three – which judging by most three-year-olds I know couldn't have made the process any easier. But every mother knows the suckling has to come to an end. The mother is beginning to have nightmare visions of the future – involving teenage children. It has just got to stop!

So battle commences: the child, for the first time in her life, is being denied her comfort from her mother, the centre of her universe. She frets, she worries, she has a tantrum or two and she sulks. And it is painful for the mum to watch . . . It is so tempting to give in to the crying and whinging, but it has got to be done. So through removal of the mother's milk and replacement with more solid nosh, the child – often against her wishes – is weaned. Eventually it happens and the battle is over. The child sleeps through the night without the comfort of a feed from her mum. She can now sit and eat with the family. She is no longer a baby.

And amazingly the child is no longer angry with Mum, but she goes to her and has a cuddle – she snuggles into the very bosom she grieved for. Do you see? She is weaned on her mother – not from her. This is a wonderful illustration of what has happened to the soul of the psalmist and what must happen to us too.

We need to be weaned off the world

When we become Christians we are not speedily weaned from the things that used to give us pleasure. Like the small child we can be petulant, uneasy and sulky. Maybe in our hearts a little voice murmurs:

> But I like being self-seeking;
> I like being materialistic;
> I like drinking too much alcohol;
> I like overindulging my senses in good things;
> I like gossiping.

The list could go on and on and on.

But it is a real sign of spiritual growth when we stop raging and kicking against our heavenly Father, when we stop longing for things that once seemed so essential, and we turn for comfort to the one who is weaning us. When we finally say, 'I don't need those things any more.'

And it is not that we become like robokids who don't need feeding at all. No, we are still hungry. A weaned soul still longs for happiness and fulfilment, but it no longer seeks happiness in worldly things. It looks to its heavenly Father and depends completely on his strength, his providing everything we need and his grace to fill us up.

We are weaned on to the Lord

The true secret of happiness and fulfilment is to be content with what you have *today*, where you are placed today.

A Puritan wrote: 'Contentment comes not from getting more but from wanting less – wanting only the things that God chooses to give us.'[4] Wise words, particularly for us living as we do in a society where there is so much affluence and excess of everything.

If we ministers' wives don't learn contentment pretty quickly, our houses will always be too small, too big, too old, too modern, too avocado. Most of us will be on a tighter budget than our friends. If we don't learn contentment then we're always going to be resentful and grasping.

If we don't learn contentment

- we will resent giving of our time to the church
- we will resent how much time our husbands spend 'doing ministry'
- we will resent giving money
- we will resent opening up our homes to others

If we are not content with our lives as Christians, we will long for the days when we were pagans, free to do as we pleased with our time and money. We will kick and scream like the unweaned child, for the pleasures the world offers us. We won't like what we have become. In fact we will hate the whole minister's wife thing.

And do you see the connection here with our pride? We will never be content if we are not humble. We will never be happy with what we have today if we have not got a right measure of ourselves. If we think we deserve better and that people ought to treat us with more respect or that we really are not in the sort of church that can use our gifts, we will never be content.

We will be like the nightmare child who just refuses to be weaned. Or like my daughter . . . One day when she was tiny I made the fatal mistake in a sleepless haze of giving her a dummy. It is one of those things, like the first time you plucked your eyebrows, when you wish you could reverse time and never do it again.

Anyway, this may not be your experience with your child, but my daughter became a confirmed addict. At the height of her addiction she could have two dummies in her mouth and one in each hand. Being a wimp – I couldn't bite the bullet – I got her down to one at night, but I just couldn't face the prospect of binning them completely, even though her teeth stuck out like a badly tended graveyard, even though she was developing a lisp. I couldn't quite face the prospect . . . Then one summer on a CYFA camp we finally did it. I took no dummies with us, so she had to break the habit.

Anyway, the point is that this meant there were still dummies lying around the house when we got back, and she could always sniff them out at a hundred yards. So for about a month I'd hear a little voice saying, 'Mummy, I've found a dummy!', and then she would roar with laughter and go charging off to find a quiet corner to have a good chomp before I found her and retracted the offending item. And all hell was let loose when I finally prised it out of her mouth. She hadn't really broken the habit – she still longed for her dummy.

Well, so it is with us if we don't daily ask God's Spirit to fill us up with humility and true contentment. The old appetites will sneak back, and we'll start seeking our happiness in worldly things again – *but they never do deliver, do they?*

I'm a shopper and I still think when I see that black top, 'That's it!' That is the top that will finally make me beautiful, acceptable, five stone lighter, and then there's the thrill of the (purr)chase: I have spending power, I am an independent woman, I have an Evans card. And I get the top home and it's not that great, and I suddenly remember the other eight black tops I already have and I feel deflated, ashamed, depressed – time for some chocolate, and so on we go.

If only we would remember that the world doesn't fulfil us. If only we could turn daily to the Lord and believe him when he says:

> Come to me, all you who are weary and burdened, and I will give you rest. Take my yoke upon you and learn from me, for I am gentle and humble in heart, and you will find rest for your souls. For my yoke is easy and my burden is light.
> (Matthew 11:28–30)

And if only we could copy Paul:

> I have learned the secret of being content in any and every situation, whether well fed or hungry, whether living in plenty or in want. I can do everything through him who gives me strength.
> (Philippians 4:12b–13)

And so, like Paul, the psalmist had learned the secret of contentment and he longed for others to do the same. In Psalm 131:3 he says, 'O Israel, put your hope in the Lord.'

It is obvious now that the way to be weaned off our self-love and our love of the visible world is to fix our sights on the treasure that is to come: our invisible hope, that hope of seeing the Lord face to face. We need to make room in our hearts for eternity by kicking out our love of transient things.

Don't you wish you could genuinely hold to this man's view of his life? He could say: 'I have sent before me all my goods into another country and am shortly for removing. And when I look about me I see a bare empty house – my treasure is in heaven. I grudge the world any part of my heart. I won't give it another glance.'[5] Wow, I bet he was a puritan!

And the psalmist too knows where believers need to set their sights:

O Israel put your hope in the LORD
    both now and for evermore.
(verse 3)

Do you see, if our eyes are in the right place – looking forward to heaven – things will fall into place and we will be in the same privileged position as the psalmist, calling others to put their hope in the Lord. Isn't that what our ministry is? Calling non-Christians and Christians alike to put their trust in the Lord.

Because we're ministers' wives, people will assume we are Christians and they will be watching to see if we put our money where our mouth is. They will be listening to our conversations about our husband, our life, our family, the job, the church to see if there is any difference between us and them.

And just by listening and watching they will sense whether we are humble, content and looking forward to heaven. Or whether we are still proud and discontented, with our eyes fixed firmly on the here and now.

So as we finish looking at this psalm, we see that the Christian ministry is a great adventure: who knows what the Lord has in store for you?

My challenge to you from this tiny psalm is to adorn yourself with a life that is really humble and content and full of hope.

For further reflection or action

1. How does thinking about who you are in God's eyes burst your pride?
2. What has contentment got to do with humility? How does Psalm 131 help you to see the connection?
3. What is the route to being weaned off the world? Turn your answer into prayer.

10. Ten questions younger ministers' wives ask (or wish they could ask)

by Rachel Lawrence

Rachel has been married to Mark for twenty-one years. They met while they were both at university: Rachel was studying nursing and Mark's degree was in biomedical sciences. During their time in London Mark was President of the Christian Union at St Thomas' Hospital and Rachel was the secretary. After going out together for three years, they married in 1989 and moved to start a new life together in Bristol.

From early on in their friendship Rachel was aware that eventually Mark would end up being a full-time minister of the gospel. After university he worked for six years for a high-street bank in the retail and corporate sectors, at the same time serving as pastoral assistant on the eldership at Kensington Baptist Church. Eventually in 1995 he was ordained as a full-time minister and became assistant pastor for five years alongside the pastor, Andy Paterson. In 2000 Mark received a call to become senior pastor at West Street Baptist Church & Christian Centre in Dunstable, Bedfordshire.

Rachel had qualified as a health visitor in 1992 before giving birth to their three children, Anna, Peter and Tom. As a wife and mother she has always combined serving as a pastor's wife with working part-time. At present she works as a specialist health visitor for children with disabilities. However, what she enjoys best is running the women's ministry at West Street, and over the years it has been wonderful to see the work grow as individuals have come to faith.

Relaxation for Rachel includes playing the piano, acting as goal defence in the church netball team and enjoying board games with her youngest son.

Author's note regarding the questions: The questions that I have been asked all come from wives of newly ordained ministers in churches across the UK. Roughly half the questions come from wives in Anglican evangelical churches and half from FIEC (Fellowship of Independent Evangelical Churches) church contexts. In total I received over thirty questions to answer and have addressed as wide a range of these as is possible in the space provided.

Questions about being an assistant minister's wife

Q1. My husband is about to become an assistant minister. What should my aims be?

Much of the answer to this has been covered in the book: about guarding your marriage or about using your gifts. But here are two foundational aims for this stage of life:

a. Develop and strengthen your relationship with God

Whatever else you are doing, do that. It is not about what we do, but who we are as we walk with our Lord and Saviour Jesus Christ which will form the foundation of our ministry. During difficult times it will be your own personal assurance of faith and the fact that you have been called by God to serve alongside your husband as his wife that will carry you through. There have been times in my own life when I have been able to do very little in the life of the church, for various reasons. Having small children was a significant limiting factor in itself for me, but I have tried to keep my main aims (with varying degrees of success) as being a godly helper to my husband and enjoying being a believer. For me on a practical level, this has involved setting the pace of my own life at a sustainable level where I have time to grow in my relationship with God. The temptation for me has always been to use every last bit of energy and time 'doing' at the expense of growing as a Christian. As you start your ministry make sure you guard your relationship with the Lord, remembering that this is your highest calling which is at the heart of your ministry life.

b. Love the church (by which I mean the people, not the architecture!)

The type of church you are serving might be considerably different from where you worshipped before. For example, you might be more used to belonging to a large city church where there are lots of families, but now you find yourself serving in a more rural area where the local branch of Fat Face is miles away and the congregation is much more diverse than what you have been used to. How they educate their children or how they shop may be very different from the way you do things, and they may have much higher (or lower) aspirations for family life and children. You may feel that they live life differently from you and furthermore you may be more aware of these differences than the congregation or even your husband. It is not at all surprising that the first few months in your new church can lead to your feeling rather out of your depth, with perhaps a degree of 'homesickness' as you adjust. Do not allow any room for snobbery (inverted or otherwise!). This is when you need consciously to decide to 'love the church' and trust God's providence in your life by remembering that God has called your husband to gospel ministry in this particular town. Adapting to perceived cross-cultural ministry is as important in serving a church in your own country as it would be overseas.

Don't panic but enjoy the process of getting to know people in any way you can. In my own experience I have often been surprised about how fulfilling an unlikely looking relationship can become. If you are younger you may well find that you build relationships first with those who are at a similar life stage to yourself (especially if you have young children). Yet do try to get alongside those who are older than you; some of the most rewarding relationships that I have within our church are with older women who have come to be my role models over the ten years we have been here. There is one woman in particular who is nearly eighty who always encourages me when we chat together. She is one of life's bright stars and has loved the Lord ever since she was in her teens, serving him faithfully all these years. She is such an example to me of self-giving and sacrificial service, and I am very grateful to God for my friendship with her. By loving the church you will be ministered to yourself. That is how God intended it to be. Go for it and enjoy it!

Q2. My husband is part of a team ministry. Do you have any tips about relating to others on the team?

Your relationship with the other leaders in the church is important and it must be positive and constructive. Your husband needs you to get on with his senior colleagues.

Most assistant ministers realize that they have to be the senior minister's rear gunner, defending and supporting him, and this applies to their wives too. There will be times when you will hear criticism of the senior minister or team members, and it is vital that you recognize your responsibility to support and back the leadership. This is something we all have to learn early in our ministry lives in order to promote unity in the church, and that includes unity within the leadership team. Hopefully this all goes without saying. However, it can catch us unawares, particularly in the early months in a church when we are not fully conversant with the underlying politics that can exist within church life.

Ideally you will need to welcome opportunities to get to know others in the leadership team. Hopefully close friendships will grow and develop and become a source of mutual support. Again it comes back to the importance of building relationships. Most probably the leaders will have no expectations of you other than to be a friendly, committed church member who loves the Lord and seeks to honour him. Their responsibility to oversee the church is an enormous one, and they deserve our support and respect.

Trust your husband's boss in the training of your husband. That is what he is there for. Don't take offence when he critiques your husband's preaching or leading. Ultimately your husband needs this input in his ministry, and it doesn't help him if you resent it or if you criticize his senior colleague. It is also worth saying that the senior minister's wife doesn't need you to criticize her husband to her either, as she will certainly be aware of his weaknesses and failings!

Q3. What do you do if you discover that relationships within the leadership team are not as good as you had hoped they would be?

This is obviously far from ideal but unfortunately can be a reality in many pastoral situations. Your challenge will then be how to react in a godly way to these pressures. As an assistant's wife it really is not your role to barge in and try to sort things out. Much more will be gained by a quiet manner which honours the Lord and maintains your own dignity. Make sure it is your husband's role to say anything if it needs to be said at all. A useful rule of thumb here is this: would you phone your husband's Senior Manager if he worked for a secular company to complain about his pay and working conditions? Of course you would not. However, the temptation in church life where relationships are much more open and intertwined is sometimes for wives to want to say things that are actually less than helpful. Guard your heart from bitterness and resentment by praying regularly for the leadership, and encourage your husband by being as positive as you can, to enable him to get on with the job that needs to be done.

Q4. My husband's assistantship is coming to an end, and we are moving to a new job where he will be in charge. Do you have any advice?

Yes, decide to enjoy the whole process!

a. Reflect and give thanks for what is past

Consider and give thanks for the relationships that you have built at your current church. Some of these are likely to have been really positive, and it will be sad to say 'goodbye'. Our husbands will be very excited about the prospect of moving on, but often wives find it harder to move on emotionally. The situation you found so strange at the beginning will now be so much part of you. Relationships that you originally thought would be so hard to establish are now deep and meaningful, and you face moving on and starting all over again. You need to see God's purpose for your move in the light of his 'big picture': the spread of the gospel. It isn't always easy, but God will help you if you allow him. Pray too for your children as they make the move.

For some of you moving on may be a big relief. Not every assistantship or curacy is a happy one, and maybe you have struggled with some relationships. In your quiet moments you may be well aware of mistakes that you have made. I think most of us would reflect on years of ministry and spot issues that we would have dealt with differently. If this is the case then use the opportunity of moving on to make a fresh start and learn from your previous experiences. Spend some time praying about what is past. Give thanks to God for the opportunities he has given you, but be honest enough with yourself to confess your weakness and failures before the Lord, and then firmly put the past behind you. He, mercifully, is so gracious and wants to teach us.

b. Look forward to what is to come

Moving on will be a big challenge both physically and emotionally, and huge amounts of humour will be needed to counteract the stress of moving house and kids, as well as your husband! Once you start, life will be extremely busy. When we moved to Dunstable, Mark faced a range of new challenges in those first few months. For a start we had left a team ministry in Bristol, and suddenly he was working alone for several months until the church called an assistant to join the pastoral team. The volume of work was considerable at times as he was preaching three times a week while leading the church through a time of real change and getting to know his new congregation. I found I needed high energy levels just to keep the house running and in order to listen to him as he was absorbing his new surroundings. As I write this I have to say that life hasn't changed very much, even though he now has two assistants! Ministry will always grow to capacity. However, being married to a pastor means you are likely to spend many evenings without your husband and you will hear about difficult situations. Keeping your own schedule reasonably calm so that you are able to take up the slack at home and support your husband practically during this busy phase will be very important.

Regarding your own ministry, work out what you want to do in your church, having evaluated your input over the last few years in your present position. Plan carefully how much you are going to take on, and resist the temptation to get involved with everything all at once. There will be plenty of opportunity in the years to come for you gradually to extend your ministry if that is what you believe is right.

Q5. How do you keep going when you become unsure as to whether or not this is the right path for you?

I don't think it is very surprising if you are feeling this in the early days of ministry.

Many of you will have experienced big life changes in the run-up to commencing ministry together. Probably you will be serving in a new town, having to make new friends and possibly settle children into new schools. Some degree of anxiety or sense of 'what have we done?' is not surprising. My advice is to take each day as it comes and encourage your husband as he grows and develops in his role. There is no other job like it, and it will take time for him to learn and to cultivate a degree of confidence.

Many ministers have a sense of calling when entering the ministry. However, I am also aware that some wives would express concern at the use of this phrase because they themselves have never felt this in any strong way, but have simply followed the path that their husbands are taking. For some the concept of 'going into the ministry' was not part of family expectations at the time of marriage, and the wife has to make the decision either to fight it or support her husband. The issue of being 'called' into the ministry is a frequent subject within other publications and it might be useful to read round this topic. However, the main issue that a new minister's wife needs to grasp is that if this is the right path for her husband *then it is also the right path for her*. Your sense of it 'feeling right' will grow over a period of time as you watch your husband enjoy his job, see his gifts develop, and as the congregation affirm his calling by growing spiritually and allowing him to minister to them.

In the meantime concentrate on developing your relationships within the church, and where you are able serve faithfully. I love the verse that links service with assurance of faith (1 Timothy 3:13). Through living faithfully and serving we grow in our faith, and the feelings part will follow on.

However, I think it is important for you to develop your life outside the church family too. Make sure you keep in touch with old friends from previous church situations or Bible college. They will be able to support you as a couple in the early months. Watch out for feelings of resentment or bitterness in your marriage. If you are really struggling with the decision your husband has made to enter the ministry then talk to him about it and get some wise advice. Generally these feelings will disappear as you settle into your new church family (which can take a while) and as you relax into your new life.

Questions about life at home

Q6. How do I encourage my husband in a constructive way to be more godly?

Pastors, like every husband, will go through periods of discouragement and disillusionment and possibly spiritually dry times. As wives we need to remember that we are their partners in good times and bad, and our reaction during these times is integral in helping them through. You may well be the only person who knows how difficult your husband is finding things and you are the only person who can pray knowledgeably for him. Your own mood can easily be affected at these times, and you need to pray that God will meet with him and encourage him. In the early years of their ministry many pastors doubt their own ability to preach as well as they would really like to, or to handle difficult situations within church life. Sometimes they have to cope with intense criticism of their ministry and can find themselves markedly lacking the confidence to do the job. Your role is to pray for your husband, to be emotionally and physically close to him and to keep the routine of home life going in order to relieve some of the pressure on him.

Learn to make encouragement a weekly by-product of your marriage. Find something good to say about your husband's sermon on the day he preaches it, and tell him what you have learned; keep any constructive criticism until the middle of the week. Remember during church services that how he preaches is not your responsibility. It is not for you to find fault with the sermon or how he presents himself. Leave his training to his senior ministry partner and pray that God will speak to you through the ministry of your husband.

There may be times when your toes curl in embarrassment during his sermons, but this is probably much more to do with your state of hyperawareness than anything he says or does. Over a lifetime the bulk of your spiritual food is going to come through your husband, so learn to enjoy his unique way of teaching the Bible, minimizing your critique of him. Your husband really needs you to encourage him, and at times your encouragement will be crucial in keeping him going.

Free him up to attend fraternals and conferences. Even if your children are small, enrol grandparents or 'adopted' grandparents from within the church to assist you and enable him to meet up with his ministry colleagues for spiritual and social refreshment. Accountability groups may also be a good idea if he has the opportunity. We need to understand that how we respond to him taking time out will influence his enjoyment and enthusiasm for joining with other ministers. Don't begrudge him this sort of opportunity, as he will greatly benefit from the encouragement of sharing with other pastors. And a warm, welcome home with the implication that life has carried on happily without him will encourage him to go away again.

To summarize, remember that your husband's sanctification is God's work. So if you are worried about him pray for him, lots. Wonderfully, God has given you to your husband to be his helper and God will use you to encourage him.

Throughout our years in ministry we have seen some very sad situations when ministers and their wives have really begun to struggle, and a few have had to give up on account of marriages that have failed. Just because we are in ministry does not make us exempt from real difficulties in our marriages, families or churches. However, the unique challenge we face is where we go for help. If you are really worried about your husband or your marriage, make sure you access some good, confidential advice: talk to your senior colleagues if that is appropriate or choose some very trusted friends outside the church situation. I know that the FIEC has a confidential helpline (see the list of websites etc. at the end of the book) which might be useful, and many dioceses would also be able to point you in the right direction. Whatever you do, don't delay in getting help.

Q7. How much should I share with my husband (and vice versa) about people in the church?

First, do not expect your husband to tell you everything that he hears. This would clearly be inappropriate as people will rightly expect him to respect their confidentiality. Certainly do not *seek* private information – the longer you are in ministry the more you realize that not knowing something can be really helpful.

Secondly, never box yourself in by promising total confidentiality to those whom you are caring for. If you sense things are getting deep and meaningful then have the common sense to interject and say, 'I am not sure what you are about to tell me, but I cannot promise you confidentiality – I might want to talk to my husband about it.' This then does protect you from listening to stuff which clearly needs dealing with or might have significant safety issues for others.

However, I am aware that some couples believe that there should be complete openness between them to the extent that what is shared with the husband can, and some say 'should', always be shared with his wife. The underlying philosophy of this model is that if trust is complete within the marriage then all confidentialities can (and possibly *should*) be shared.

But I think this model can be problematic for a number of reasons. First of all it breaches the accepted code of confidentiality reasonably expected by the congregation of a minister. When I visit my GP I expect confidentiality from him, and even if I know his wife I would not wish my details to be discussed with her. Similarly, if I speak to my children's teachers I wouldn't expect them to go home and discuss my child with their spouse. When people talk to my husband he promises them that what they say will remain confidential unless (a) he feels it would help him or the person he is counselling for it to be shared in confidence with me or someone on his pastoral team, in which case he will always ask permission or (b) there is an explicit reason why confidentiality cannot be promised, such as safeguarding children or a vulnerable person or another third party.

Secondly, if I regard my husband's keeping of a confidence from me as him 'not trusting me', I am placing a pressure on my marriage and his role as a pastor that in my view is unsustainable. Particularly in a larger church the quantity of information that requires very careful handling is huge, and there need to be some boundaries. In our situation Mark regularly meets with men in the congregation, and I cannot imagine how they would feel if they thought that what they shared with him was then told to me. And I do know that my friendships would become strained if I told Mark everything that was shared with me!

Speaking more generally, in our experience people often say to me, 'Please feel free to tell Mark this', and he is often asked or given permission to tell me things (e.g. if news of a pregnancy is shared at an early stage). Very often members of your congregation will want you *both* to know what is going on in their lives so that you are aware of what they are going through and can pray for them accordingly. Showing a genuine interest in people's lives is one of the greatest privileges of Christian ministry but also one of the greatest responsibilities. It goes without saying that your congregation need to know that between you as a couple information is then kept confidential.

Handling confidential information can sometimes make you feel that you need a degree in diplomacy as you engage with your congregation, and this can be quite stressful at times. There have been many occasions when Mark has not told me about specific situations purely because it makes life easier for me as I mingle with the congregation. When you are party to confidential information, learn to 'tag it' in your mind so that you avoid compromising other people or embarrassing your husband. If in doubt, always veer on the side of refusing to share what you know. Be aware too that there will always be some people who will try to probe and test what you or your husband know and whose approaches need to be skilfully deflected.

Q8. How do you get the right balance of encouraging your husband to be diligent and thorough in his preparation of sermons, while at the same time not spending hours 'finessing' a sermon at the expense of family time?

This can be a very hard balance to achieve. Most experienced preachers will tell you that in the early years sermon preparation takes a massive amount of time. Indeed, it is the heart of a pastor's job alongside prayer. It is vital that you do not see thorough sermon preparation by your husband as 'time away from the family'.

It is tempting to set 'preparation time' against 'the family', and I think this is a big issue for new ministry couples especially. It can appear as if the two issues are directly opposed to each other, particularly if your husband's study is at home. Our logic as wives can become: 'If only you were quicker at writing your sermons then we could spend more time together as a family!' The tension can then ratchet up as you gently push for your husband to spend less time finishing his sermon late into the evening and more time with the family (or you!).

It is very important that adequate time is taken to allow a merely 'competent' sermon to be transformed into a prayerfully prepared sermon which when preached and applied in the power of the Holy Spirit may reach the hearts and minds of all the congregation. Therefore what to you might seem like 'finessing' a sermon is most probably the crucial part of sermon prep that brings it to life. Sermon preparation is much more an art than a science, and the last ten per cent of preparation is frequently crucial. This is something worth talking through as a couple with your senior colleagues as they will have been through this too.

However, I am also aware that sermon preparation can sometimes be a work that is never done which 'expands to fill all the time available'. It is sometimes necessary for boundaries to be put in place in order for the whole family to survive the process. Just as your husband needs to set up good working habits during the week to ensure his preparation is done in time, so we wives need to be flexible and manage our own expectations.

I think that the challenge in ministry life is that in normal, day-to-day church life there are many calls on your husband's time, and preparation time for sermons is regularly disturbed or diverted by real pastoral issues. The challenge is not to take this personally but to free him up to do the job he is set aside to do.

The reality in ministry is that boundaries between 'work' and 'play' are often very hard to define. The ministry is not a nine-to-five job but rather a whole-life experience. You can mistakenly respond to this by veering to extremes. Either you try to construct rigid time boundaries which inhibit his growth in ministry and do not serve the church, or by allowing no separation between public ministry and private family life you risk causing your marriage and family life to be stunted and even damaged. On the one hand we are the only ones who will 'fight' for the corner of our families and marriages, but we need to be careful that our encouragement to spend more time at home is not seen by our husbands as counterproductive nagging.

Obviously we will want the church to be sacrificially served, our husbands' ministries to grow and develop, and family life to be strong. So make sure you really enjoy your time off together in whatever form that takes.

Your husband may well experience times when he needs to burn the midnight oil to work through a sermon, and it is often these sermons which the Lord uses and particularly blesses. Don't be frightened of freeing up your husband to put in the hours necessary; make sure you are not acting as a barrier to his preaching ministry developing. As he gains more experience he will speed up or at the very least will learn to judge more accurately how long preparation will take him.

This is something that needs to be continually reviewed in your ministry life together. Commit it to the Lord and don't be afraid to talk about it from time to time with older pastors' wives.

Q 9. How do we reduce the risk of our children becoming 'rebel vicar's kids'?

The idea of the 'rebel vicar's kid' is a caricature and thankfully is much more associated with media representation than anything to do with the gospel. However, the question is asked from the heart, and it is certainly one pondered by many parents in full-time Christian work.

It is really important not to expect this stereotype to unfold with your own children. Our desire for our children to become Christians is the same as that of any committed Christian parents. We all pray for our children from the very beginning that they will respond to the gospel in repentance and faith. Mercifully it is the Lord's work in our children's life that ultimately will determine how our children respond to the gospel, and we need to be very clear about that. How we parent is obviously important, yet this is so too for any committed Christian parents, and there is absolutely no reason why having parents who serve in the ministry should cause our children to react against the gospel.

We must bring up our children in faith, not fear, and we need to be confident that it is not only possible for our kids to enjoy being part of a ministry home but it is also an immense privilege for them. That is borne out by the number of pastors' children going into the ministry themselves. How our children react to being part of a ministry family is down to how we respond to gospel realities in our own lives and how we manage our expectations of our children. The love and enthusiasm with which we talk about the ministry and the church during their childhood will have a direct effect on their own love for the Lord and his people: if *we* love the church then *they* are likely to grow up loving the community of God's people. If the church too is properly demonstrating God's grace then they will experience and witness a whole range of gospel truths in action.

There are many joys to being part of a ministry home. By comparison with the average Joe Public, ministry children have a wide-ranging social life; they learn to relate to a large number of people from different backgrounds and frequently enjoy many and varied church activities. Our own children have met and had lunch with numerous ministers and their families over the years; they are used to having frequent visitors in the home, and I am in no doubt that they have benefited immensely from regular contact with a caring and considerate congregation.

If necessary, get involved yourself in the children's ministry to make it the best you can possibly make it. Take advantage of youth groups in other Bible-believing churches to widen their social interaction with other Christians of their age, particularly if your fellowship is smaller; it is vital that as they grow older you enable them to see that the Christian church is bigger than just your own fellowship. We are very privileged to have many excellent youth camps here in the UK, and it is good to make full use of them. (Our two eldest children have loved being part of, and greatly benefited from, the Contagious Bible-centred youth conference which is run in partnership with the FIEC.)

Spare your children the details of church politics, and always speak of the blessings and encouragements of your church situation. Of course your children may observe comings and goings in your home, and it's good to explain that what they see and may sometimes overhear should stay strictly within the home. But if you feel that this is asking too much of them, especially while they are younger, then it's your job to protect them from this responsibility. Similarly you need to protect their privacy from the gaze of others as your family shares its life within the congregation.

While talking about the benefits of ministry family life, I realize that you may be in the position where it seems to you that your child is showing no desire to walk with the Lord. This is hard for any Christian parent to come to terms with and it calls for ongoing prayer and trust in our gracious God to bring them face to face, by faith, with the risen Jesus Christ.

Q10. Is it possible to be a minister's wife while working outside the home and church environment?

It takes all sorts to be a minister's wife. Increasingly, many families have to rely on two incomes to repay even a modest mortgage, and ministry families are no different from the norm. Recently the pressure on families to contribute to university fees has made paid work an almost inevitable reality for women with teenage children. I think that the days of expecting the wife to work full-time in the church are largely gone (thank goodness!), and just as other women will decide to work outside the home, so ministers' wives for whatever reasons will choose to do the same.

Combining work and home responsibilities along with church responsibilities makes life interesting and sometimes quite daunting, but it is something that I have always managed to do and enjoy. When Mark was first in ministry I was working part-time as a health visitor, and I have always continued to do this to some degree or other.

For me, working outside the home has always been positive. I greatly enjoy what I do and when I have got the number of hours right my job has always been a real blessing to me. I value being myself at work and engaging with non-Christians. My day-to-day experiences enrich our home life. I think my daughter is seeing a positive image of combining motherhood and career, my husband is kept up to date with the inner workings of the NHS (!), and overall my sanity levels are generally improved by this addition to my life.

However, I am *not* saying that all pastors' wives should be working outside the home. For some it would clearly not be appropriate, or their chosen career would entail a huge commitment that could easily prove impractical or detrimental to their husband's responsibilities. For others it would not be something that they would want to do at all. The key thing is to weigh up your family's needs with the aim above all of being a good and supportive wife and mother and wherever possible to be a blessing and encouragement to women in your church and surrounding community.

For my part I have found that part-time work can be very beneficial to my sense of well-being, thereby increasing the sustainability of ministry life. It can greatly help in keeping the pressures of ministry life in perspective, as well as providing the opportunity to live and work alongside people in your community who do not yet know the Lord. When relationships and situations in church may threaten to become too intense, it can be very helpful to escape to the wider world on a Thursday morning or whatever!

If you are keen to have a job of your own outside home and church life, I recommend that you weigh carefully why you want to work and how this would impact on your husband's ministry as well as your own. My highlight of the week is running a women's Bible study ministry and overseeing the team who assist me in this, and I enjoy meeting with women during the week for coffee or being available for them as need arises. So my paid NHS work is limited to allow me time to serve in these ways. Just this morning I was walking home with our assistant minister's wife after a session where over seventy women had been studying 1 Corinthians chapter 2. She turned to me and said, 'Nothing could be more exciting than witnessing all those women studying God's Word together and getting to grips with the power of the cross.' She was absolutely right.

Others of us will have different responsibilities and will shape our lives accordingly. It is important to remember that it is not more or less 'biblical' to engage in work outside home and church life; God gives us freedom in these matters. However, the motivation behind such work needs to be biblically consistent and godly, and we should support one another in family life as we choose different options in this area.

Keep the main thing the main thing: nurture your relationship with your Lord and Saviour, love and support your husband, love and care for your children, and serve the church family as you are able with the love of Christ.

And may God bless you richly.

Further reading

On being a minister's wife

Peter Brain, *Going the Distance: How to Stay Fit for a Lifetime of Ministry* (Matthias Media, 2004).

Kent and Barbara Hughes, *Liberating Ministry from the Success Syndrome* (Crossway, 2008).

H. B. London and Neil B. Wiseman, *Married to a Pastor: How to Stay Happily Married in the Ministry* (Regal, 1999).

Gail MacDonald, *High Call, High Privilege: A Pastor's Wife Speaks to Every Woman in a Place of Responsibility* (Hendrickson, 1998).

Mary Somerville, *One With a Shepherd: The Tears and Triumphs of Ministry Marriage* (Kress Christian Publications, 2005).

On womanhood

Barbara Hughes, *The Disciplines of a Godly Woman* (Crossway, 2001).

Sharon James, *God's Design for Women: Biblical Womanhood for Today* (Evangelical Press, 2007).

Mary Kassian, *Girls Gone Wise in a World Gone Wild* (Moody Publishers, 2010).

Carolyn Mahaney, *Feminine Appeal: Seven Virtues of a Godly Wife and Mother* (Crossway, 2004).

On marriage and family

Christopher Ash, *Married for God: Making Your Marriage the Best It Can Be* (IVP, 2007).

Ann Benton, *Aren't They Lovely When They're Asleep: Lessons in Unsentimental Parenting* (Christian Focus, 2007).

Ann Benton, *If It's Not Too Much Trouble: The Challenge of the Aged Parent* (Christian Focus, 2007).

Ann Benton, *Teenagers: Biblical Wisdom for Parents* (IVP, 2009).

John and Ann Benton, *Don't They Make a Lovely Couple?* (Christian Focus, 2005).

Robert Lewis and William Hendricks, *Rocking the Roles: Building a Win-Win Marriage* (Navpress, 1999).

Louise Morse and Roger Hitchings, *Could It Be Dementia? Losing Your Mind Doesn't Mean Losing Your Soul* (Monarch, 2008).

Paul David Tripp, *What Did You Expect? Redeeming the Realities of Marriage* (IVP, 2010).

On counselling, hospitality and personal work with women

Gordon Cheng, *Encouragement: How Words Change Lives* (Matthias Media, 2006).

Tim Chester, *You Can Change: God's Transforming Power for Our Sinful Behaviour and Negative Emotions* (IVP, 2008).

Elyse Fitzpatrick and Carol Cornish, *Women Helping Women: A Biblical Guide to Issues Women Face* (Harvest House, 1997).

Julia Jones, *A Cup of Cold Water* (Day One, 2006).

Sophie Peace, *One-to-One: A Discipleship Handbook* (Authentic, 2003).

Paul David Tripp, *Instruments in the Redeemer's Hands: People in Need of Change Helping People in Need of Change* (Presbyterian & Reformed, 2002).

Edward T. Welch, *When People Are Big and God Is Small: Overcoming Peer Pressure, Codependency, and the Fear of Man* (Evangelical Press, 2007).

On forgiveness

Timothy S. Lane and Paul David Tripp, *Relationships: A Mess Worth Making* (Evangelical Press, 2010).

Dr Alfred J. Poirier, 'The Cross and Criticism': http://www.peacemaker.net/site/c.aqKFLTOBIpH/b.958163/k.AD04/Key_Articles.htm

David Powlison, *Seeing With New Eyes: Counseling and the Human Condition Through the Lens of Scripture* (Evangelical Press, 2003).

Ken Sande, 'Charitable Judgments: An Antidote to Judging Others': http://www.peacemaker.net/site/c.aqKFLTOBIpH/b.958163/k.AD04/Key_Articles.htm

Eric Wright, *A Guide to Revolutionary Forgiveness: Developing a Forgiving Lifestyle* (Evangelical Press, 2003).

On inspiring women

Darlene Deibler Rose, *Evidence Not Seen: A Woman's Miraculous Faith in the Jungles of World War II* (Authentic, 1995).

Sharon James, *Elizabeth Prentiss: More Love to Thee* (Banner of Truth, 2006).

Sharon James, *In Trouble and in Joy: Four Women Who Lived for God* (Evangelical Press, 2005).

Sharon James, *My Heart in His Hands: Ann Judson of Burma* (Evangelical Press, 1999).

On Christian living more generally

Arthur Bennett (ed.), *The Valley of Vision: A Collection of Puritan Prayers and Devotions* (Banner of Truth, 2003).

Jerry Bridges, *The Discipline of Grace: God's Role and Our Role in the Pursuit of Holiness* (Navpress, 1994).

Don Carson, *A Call to Spiritual Reformation: Priorities from Paul and His Prayers* (IVP, 1992).

Julian Hardyman, *Maximum Life: All for the Glory of God* (IVP, 2009).

Marcus Honeysett, *Finding Joy: A Radical Rediscovery of Grace* (IVP, 2005).

Helen Roseveare, *Living Faith: Willing to Be Stirred as a Pot of Paint* (Christian Focus, 2007).

Helen Roseveare, *Living Fellowship: Willing to Be the Third Side of a Triangle* (Christian Focus, 2008).

Helen Roseveare, *Living Holiness: Willing to Be the Legs of a Galloping Horse* (Christian Focus, 2008).

Helen Roseveare, *Living Sacrifice: Willing to Be Whittled as an Arrow* (Christian Focus, 2007).

Paul David Tripp, *A Shelter in the Time of Storm: Meditations on God and Trouble* (IVP, 2004).

Useful websites and organizations

Conferences:
The Proclamation Trust runs conferences annually for ministers' wives: www.proctrust.org.uk

The FIEC (Fellowship of Independent Evangelical Churches) produces a newsletter for ministers' wives and women working in churches. This contains many useful resources and also provides information on area conferences for ministers' wives: www.fiec.org.uk

Living Leadership is a growing network of leaders, churches and supporters who are committed to training and sustaining Christian leaders for God's glory. For information on their Pastoral Refreshment conference visit www.livingleadership.org.

New Wine Women and Leadership conferences: www.new-wine.org

Helpline:

The FIEC (see above) also offers a confidential helpline which can be accessed through the FIEC office.

Blogs:

http://ministry-wives.blogspot.com
http://thevicarswife.wordpress.com

Counselling resources:

The Christian Counselling and Education Foundation offers courses and resources: www.ccef.org

Notes

1. Her responsibility to God

1. Dr D. Martyn Lloyd-Jones, *The Unsearchable Riches of Christ: An Exposition of Ephesians 3* (Baker, 1980).
2. Sharon James, *My Heart in His Hands: Ann Judson of Burma* (Evangelical Press, 1999), p. 37.
3. Marcus Honeysett, *Finding Joy: A Radical Rediscovery of Grace* (IVP, 2005), p. 24.
4. Ibid., p. 25.
5. *Autobiography of George Müller*, comp. Fred Bergen (J. Nisbet, 1906), pp. 152–154.
6. Arthur Bennett (ed.), *The Valley of Vision: A Collection of Puritan Prayers and Devotions* (Banner of Truth, 1975).
7. John Piper, *Desiring God* (IVP, 2003), pp. 170–173.
8. Neil H. Williams, *Gospel Transformation*, 2nd edn (World Harvest Mission, 2006).
9. Kris Lundgaard, *The Enemy Within: Straight Talk About the Power and Defeat of Sin* (P. & R. Publishing, 1998).
10. George Matheson, 'O Love That Wilt Not Let Me Go' (1982).
11. Steve Farrar, *Finishing Strong: Going the Distance for Your Family* (Multnomah Press, 1995), p. 6.

12. Cited in Tim Chester, *The Busy Christian's Guide to Busyness* (IVP, 2006), p. 42.

2. Her responsibility to her husband

1. See Gary Chapman, *The Five Love Languages: How to Express Heartfelt Commitment to Your Mate* (Northfield Publishing, 1995).
2. C. J. Mahaney, *Sex, Romance, and the Glory of God: What Every Christian Husband Needs to Know* (Crossway, 2005).
3. Stormie Omartian, *The Power of a Praying Wife* (Kingsway, 2001).
4. Bruce W. Thielemann, *The Wittenburg Door*, no. 36 (April–May 1977).

3. Her responsibility to her family

1. Matthew Henry, *Commentary on the Whole Bible*, unabridged version, 2nd edn (Hendrickson, 1991) on Exodus 20:12.

5. Pressure points

1. Note that Anglican clergy for example do not negotiate their salaries as the pay scale is already set, while ministers in free churches often do.

6. Her service for Christ

1. Graham Beynon, *Last Things First: Living in the Light of the Future* (IVP, 2010). p. 56.
2. Ibid., p. 57.

7. Forgiveness and forbearance

1. Peter Brain, *Going the Distance: How to Stay Fit for a Lifetime of Ministry* (Matthias Media, 2004), p. 95.
2. E. W. Wright, *The Guide to Revolutionary Forgiveness: Developing a Forgiving Lifestyle* (Evangelical Press, 2003), pp. 257–258.
3. Ken Sande, Peacemaker Ministries, 'Charitable Judgments: An Antidote to Judging Others' (http://www.peacemaker.net/site/c.aqKFLTOBIpH/b.958163/k.AD04/Key_Articles.htm).

9. Humility and contentment

1. C. H. Spurgeon, *The Treasury of David: A Commentary on the Psalms* (Evangelical Press, 2004).
2. Cited in Sinclair B. Ferguson, *In Christ Alone: Living the Gospel-Centered Life* (Evangelical Press, 2008), p. 190.
3. Taken from C. J. Mahaney, *Humility: True Greatness* (Multnomah Press, 2005).
4. Paraphrase from Jeremiah Burroughs, *Rare Jewel of Christian Contentment* (Sovereign Grace, 2001).
5. C. H. Spurgeon, *The Treasury of David: A Commentary on the Psalms* (Evangelical Press, 2004).